British History in Perspective
General Editor: Jeremy Black

THE WARS
OF THE ROSES

A. J. POLLARD

**Reader in Local History
Teesside Polytechnic**

MACMILLAN

For Richard and Edward

First published 1988 by
MACMILLAN EDUCATION LTD
Houndmills, Basingstoke, Hampshire RG21 2XS
and London
Companies and representatives
throughout the world

ISBN 0–333–40603–6 hardcover
ISBN 0–333–40604–4 paperback

A catalogue record for this book is available
from the British Library.

Printed in Hong Kong

Reprinted 1990, 1992

CONTENTS

PREFACE

This work is a discussion of what seem to me to be the important and distinctive characteristics of the Wars of the Roses. It is founded upon and reflects the work of many scholars and has had the advantage of many hours of discussion with friends and colleagues too numerous to name. On some issues it agrees with them, on others it disagrees. Any strengths it possesses owes much to them, the weaknesses are all my own. I would however like to record a special debt to the late Charles Ross, whose book under the same title will for long remain the best introductory work on the subject. And I would like to thank Jill Wren for her patient assistance in preparing the typescript for publication.

Taunton
September, 1987

For Richard and Edward

England during the Wars of the Roses

X Battles   **● TOWNS**   **□ Castles**

Table 1 THE HOUSES OF LANCASTER, YORK AND BEAUFORT

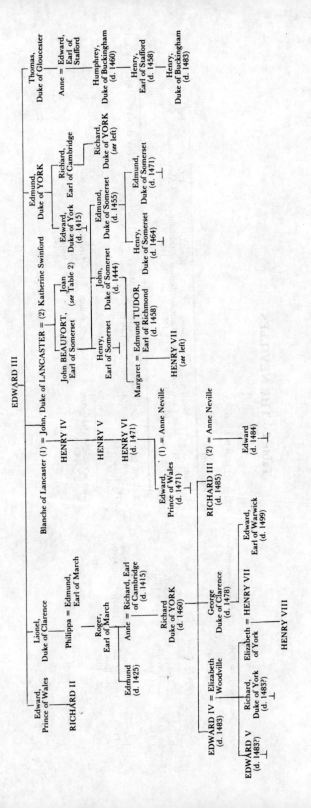

Table 2 THE NEVILLES

Margaret Stafford (1) = Ralph, 1st Earl of Westmorland (d. 1425) = (2) Joan Beaufort

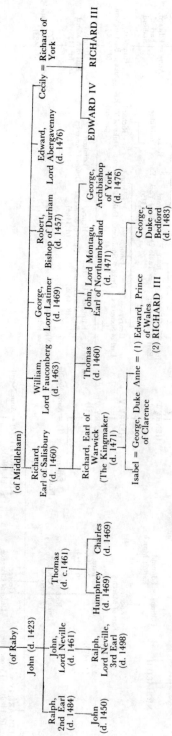

(of Raby)

John (d. 1423)

Ralph, 2nd Earl (d. 1484)

John (d. 1450)

John, Lord Neville (d. 1461)

Ralph, Lord Neville, 3rd Earl (d. 1498)

Thomas (d. c.1461)

Humphrey (d. 1469)

Charles (d. 1469)

(of Middleham)

Richard, Earl of Salisbury (d. 1460)

William, Lord Fauconberg (d. 1463)

George, Lord Latimer (d. 1469)

Robert, Bishop of Durham (d. 1457)

Edward, Lord Abergavenny (d. 1476)

Cecily = Richard of York

EDWARD IV   RICHARD III

Richard, Earl of Warwick ("The Kingmaker") (d. 1471)

Thomas (d. 1460)

John, Lord Montagu, Earl of Northumberland (d. 1471)

George, Archbishop of York (d. 1476)

George, Duke of Bedford (d. 1483)

Isabel = George, Duke of Clarence

Anne = (1) Edward, Prince of Wales
       (2) RICHARD III

INTRODUCTION

The phrase 'The Wars of the Roses' is one of those historical terms like 'The Agricultural Revolution' or 'The Glorious Revolution' which some historians would like to see thrown in the dustbin, but which nevertheless survives if only as a matter of convenience and common currency. By tradition the Wars of the Roses signify a period of total anarchy brought on by a dynastic conflict which divided England before the coming of the Tudors. Whether they are considered to have started in 1399 (as was originally the case) or in 1455 (as has been the case for the last 100 years), in common discourse they serve as a type for the worst possible civil strife and discord which has ever occurred in England and which must never be allowed to occur again. For this reason they have never quite lost their topicality. Politicians are wont to invoke the spectre of the wars as part of their propaganda. Thus the last months of the Callaghan government of 1976–79, which were plagued by a series of very visible industrial disputes, have been tagged 'The Winter of Discontent' by public figures anxious to conjure up an image of the utter chaos from which the kingdom was rescued. What more effective way was there than to draw upon the opening lines of Shakespeare's *Richard III* which refer directly to a phase of the Wars of the Roses in these terms? Moreover reference is still made to the 'overmighty' trade unions suggesting a comparison with the overmighty subjects responsible for the civil disorders of the fifteenth century.

It is not just politicians who retain a traditional and fixed idea of the Wars of the Roses. In 1977 *The Sunday Times* carried a review by Bernard Levin of Terry Hands' spectacular production of the three parts of *Henry VI* for the Royal Shakespeare Company. In his opening remarks, Levin ruminated on the likelihood that there were old people still living in Stratford when Shakespeare was born who were alive before Bosworth. The Wars of the Roses were thus not merely history: 'the air still resounded with the cries of the wounded and dying, and the earth was soaked with their blood'. For this reason, Levin suggested, 'it is hardly to be wondered at that the horror of ambition, faction and anarchy, with which he (Shakespeare) grew up, never left him'.[1] It is perhaps understandable that in 1977 Bernard Levin was not in touch with recent thought about the Wars of the Roses (or Shakespeare for that matter). But even in 1986 it was possible for one Shakespearean scholar writing on the playwright's perception of politics and history to remark in passing and without any apparent awareness of a different perspective on the 'chaos of the Wars of the Roses'.[2] In some circles, academic as well as literary and political, the Sellar and Yeatman vision of the Wars of the Roses as the revival of the 'Feudal amenities of Sackage, Carnage, and Wreckage' still remains supreme.[3]

This work is a reconsideration of the Wars of the Roses. It is both an examination of what the phrase itself has meant (and still means) as a summing up of one particular phase in English history and a discussion of what happened, why and with what consequences in the later-fifteenth century. It is a political not a military history. For recent discussions of the military history the reader can turn elsewhere, especially to the works of Anthony Goodman and Charles Ross.[4] In concentrating on the political theme the work follows K. B. McFarlane's adaptation of Clausewitz's dictum that civil war is 'the continuation of politics by other means'.[5] Chapter 2 offers a narrative, but if more detail is wanted the reader has a wide choice of modern textbooks and monographs to which to turn. The narrative here serves as a basis for the further discussion of the causes, character, scale and aftermath of the wars.

As a study in political history this work does not take up in detail a discussion of the age as a whole. To some this might seem a grave imbalance. One of the paradoxes of the age of the Wars of the Roses is that it was also, despite the characteristic dismissal of one nineteenth-century historian, an age which indeed witnessed significant 'progress in the arts of peace'.[6] The last decades of the fifteenth century were years of economic development and growing *per capita* prosperity for many men and women especially in south-eastern and south-western England. These same decades were the years when the 'New Learning' began to take root in England and the first humanist grammar school, Magdalen College School, Oxford, was founded. It was also in the middle of the Wars of the Roses that Caxton, then Oxford University and others set up their printing presses. It was an age, in fact, of expanding educational opportunity and (possibly) growing literacy, whether in the new fashion or more commonly in the traditional mould. It was perhaps also an era of intensifying personal religious devotion and piety; an era in which lay men and women in growing numbers began to demand more of the institutions of the Church than they ultimately could supply. And it was also, in the midst of civil war, the age of rebuilding in the perpendicular style of East Anglian naves and Somerset bell towers. Thus, while it is recognised that during the Wars of the Roses English society was at the same time experiencing significant cultural change ('progress in the arts of peace'), this work is not an examination of that process of renewal and resurgence itself.

If this work can claim to add a distinctive perspective to the subject it might lie in the attempt to place the experience of civil war in England in the later-fifteenth century in a wider European context. Most recent comment has tended to emphasise the fact that in comparison with the experience of neighbouring European kingdoms England suffered little from the ravages of civil war. What has tended to be overlooked is the basic fact that there was a common experience of such civil war. Approaches to the Wars of the Roses have tended to be excessively Anglocentric. The normal perspective is that of the place of the wars in the march of English history and, more recently, the unfolding of English historiography. But England in the later-fifteenth century was also part of a European community. The European context impinges on England in two ways. First of all the rulers of England were caught in a complex network of international relations. In the continual game of international politics and diplomacy the internal affairs of neighbouring kingdoms were as significant to rival powers as the external posturing. Thus all rulers, of England as well as of France, Scotland, the Burgundian inheritance or the Spanish kingdoms, intervened in the affairs of the others. Intrigue and plotting and occasional open military intervention were part and parcel of the constant attempts to destabilise and exploit the weaknesses of rivals. The civil wars of England, France, Scotland, Burgundy or Spain were all at critical times intensified and extended by foreign intervention. In an important sense the Wars of the Roses were a part of an interlinked chain of European civil wars. Secondly England and her neighbouring kingdoms were all by the very nature of their political structures and the cultural values of their élites prone to civil war. Central governments in all European kingdoms and states were fundamentally weak and lacking in coercive power. All depended on the willing obedience and cooperation of a highly volatile and independent nobility. Moreover the nobility of Europe was educated in the school of chivalry which elevated the making of war to the highest secular ideal. Civil war, therefore, was generally in northern Europe less exceptional than it seems today.

1

THE WARS IN HISTORY

The twentieth century, especially the last third, has witnessed a major revision of received ideas about the Wars of the Roses. The 30 years 1455–85, it has been argued, were neither years of constant civil strife nor years of uncontrolled anarchy. In terms of open warfare, it has often been repeated, there were no more than 12 or 13 weeks of actual fighting in the whole 30 years. And this fighting was restricted to the narrow world of the political élite, most of whose members were either indifferent to the outcome or shamelessly opportunistic. A handful of isolated battles, armed clashes, murders and executions, we are told, had little impact on the day-to-day life of the kingdom. These inconveniences were not caused by dynastic dispute: the question of the throne only arose as a consequence of political rivalry. There were no roses, red for Lancaster or white for York, deployed as badges by rival parties. Even the phrase 'Wars of the Roses', we are assured, was not thought of until invented by Sir Walter Scott.[1] In short, the Wars of the Roses is a myth. In its extreme manifestation this was the argument advanced by the late S. B. Chrimes in a recorded discussion with Professor R. L. Storey. The roses, he stated, had nothing to do with it and there were not, 'in any meaningful sense', any wars. The only admissible use of the phrase, he conceded, was if it were restricted to the first three months of 1461.[2] The Wars of the Roses, it would seem, have been talked out of existence.

Apart from the fact that it would probably be impossible to

remove the phrase from our language, there are, however, compelling historiographical grounds as well as sound historical reasons for retaining it. To start with the roses. While it may be strictly true to say that the exact phrase 'the Wars of the Roses' was not employed until the early-nineteenth century, as Dr Aston pointed out in 1971, the concept it encapsulates of the warring roses has a very long history stretching back through Hume's 'wars of the two roses' (1761) and Sir John Oglander's 'the quarrel of the warring roses' (1646) to the fifteenth century itself.[3] Badges (as has frequently been observed) were adopted individually by late-medieval noblemen and women. A great family, especially a royal family, collected several, reflecting its own lineage and agglomeration of titles from different ancestors. An individual might even use several badges reflecting different claims, associations and objectives. Henry VII deployed not only the Tudor Rose itself but also the portcullis (from his mother), the red dragon of cadwallader (from his father's line) and fleetingly a dun cow for his earldom of Richmond. Thus the house of Lancaster had a red rose in its vast collection – used more by fourteenth-century earls and dukes. While the favourite badge of the last Lancastrian, Henry VI, was an antelope, there is a likelihood that the red rose became an emblem of the Beauforts, also descended from the dukes of Lancaster. Similarly the white rose is to be found in Yorkist use (inherited from the Mortimer earls of March), but the badge of Richard of York was a falcon and fetterlock, the badge of his son Edward IV a sun with streamers, of George, duke of Clarence a black bull and of Richard III a white boar. It seems that Elizabeth of York herself took up the white rose as her personal badge; and plausible that Henry VII on coming to the throne in 1485 adopted the old, Lancastrian/Beaufort red rose of his mother for the very ease with which it could be deployed for propaganda effect.

The roses became quickly significant because of their immediate employment by Henry VII. The evidence is unambiguous. In April 1486 the new king made his first, critical progress to the north of England. So as to ensure that maximum advantage was taken of his entry into York, the region's capital, he sent ahead instructions as to how he should be received. A series of pageants and displays were to be mounted. The very first, at Micklegate Bar, through which he was to enter, was to represent a heaven 'of great joy and angelical harmony' and under it 'a world desolate full of trees and flowers' in which was to be contrived (mechanically) 'a royal, rich, red rose conveyed by a vice, unto which rose shall appear another rich white rose, unto whom all the flowers shall lout (bow) and evidently give sovereignty, showing the rose to be principal of all flowers, and there upon shall come from a cloud a crown covering the roses'. Thus was the Tudor badge of the rose and crown to be created before the very eyes of the citizens of York.[4] The message was clear and unambiguous. At approximately the same time, at the abbey of Crowland further south, a senior civil servant was putting the finishing touches to his account of the history of the Yorkist dynasty. He added some exhortatory verses, including the following lines, which he helpfully told his readers employed the banner and badges of the victor, vanquished and sons of Edward IV, whose cause was avenged.

> In the year 1485 on the 22nd day of August the tusks of the boar were blunted and the red rose, the avenger of the white, shines upon us.[5]

If the author is to be believed the roses were respectively the badges of Henry VII and the children of Edward IV and their symbolism was clearly understood by contemporaries.

The imagery and idea thus propagated became firmly established in the received wisdom of what the victorious and ultimately successful Henry VII had achieved. Thus in 1561 Sir Thomas Smith, speaking for the realm, urged Elizabeth I to marry so that she could perpetuate 'the race of the mixed rose, which brought again the amicable peace long exiled from among my children by the striving of the two roses'. And later in the same pamphlet he added more colourfully, 'those two blades of Lyonel and John of Gaunt never rested pursuing the th'one th'other, till the red rose was almost razed out, and the white made all bloody'.[6] The idea of the warring roses, if not the specific phrase, 'The Wars of the Roses', undoubtedly had contemporary origins and was elaborated within two or three generations as part of an all-embracing interpretation of the past.

That interpretation was also spelt out as early as 1486. The preamble to the papal bull of dispensation permitting the marriage of Henry VII and Elizabeth of York, the text of which was composed by the king's servants, read as follows:

> Our Holy Father, the Pope Innocent VIII, understanding of the long and grievous variance, contentions and debates that hath been in the Realm of England between the house of Lancaster on the one party and the house of York on the other party, willing all such divisions following to be put apart, by the counsel and consent of his college of cardinals approveth, confirmeth and establisheth the matrimony and conjunction made between our sovereign King Henry VII, of the house of Lancaster, of that one party and the noble Princess Elizabeth of the house of York of that other with all their issue lawfully born between the same.

The bull was published and orders issued for it to be read from every pulpit.[7]

But Henry VII was not the first usurping king to suggest that his accession would end 'the long and grievous variance'. Richard III in his parliamentary declaration of his title emphasised more luridly that during the reign of his brother Edward IV:

> no man was sure of his life, land, nor livelihood, nor of his wife, daughter, nor servant, every good maiden and woman standing in dread to be ravished and defouled. And besides this, what discords, inward battles, effusion of Christian men's blood, and namely by the destruction of the noble blood of this land, was had and committed within the same, it is evident and notorious through all this realm, unto the great sorrow and heaviness of all true Englishmen.[8]

Richard III was in fact borrowing the language used by Edward IV which he had used 22 years earlier to blacken his predecessor:

> this realm of England therefore hath suffered the charge of intolerable persecution, punishment and tribulation, whereof the like hath not been seen or heard in any other Christian realm by any memory or record, unrest, inward war and trouble, unrighteousness, shedding and effusion of innocent blood, abuse of the laws, partiality, riot, extortion, murder, rape and vicious

living, have been the guiders and leaders of the noble realm of England.[9]

Moreover, Edward IV, invoking the propaganda lately employed by his father, stated for the first time the idea that this anarchy resulted from Henry IV's heinous crime 'against God's law, man's liegance and oath of fidelity' of deposing Richard II. The *idea* of the Wars of the Roses as a period of anarchy consequent upon the deposition of Richard II indeed had its roots in contemporary propaganda: Yorkist, not Tudor, propaganda. Henry VII took it over and added the particular detail of the red and white roses as symbols of Lancaster and York.

What began as the crude propaganda of successive usurping kings was absorbed and elaborated by later generations so that by the mid-sixteenth century it had been transformed into a persuasive and sophisticated historical explanation of the past. It was taken up and developed by the early-Tudor historian Polydore Vergil in his *English History*; made more accessible in Hall's *Union of the Houses of Lancaster and York*, a mid-century celebration of the success of the Tudor dynasty; employed with a flourish by Sir Thomas Smith; and completed in Shakespeare's great cycle of history plays. By 1600 there could have been scarcely anyone in England who did not know about the Wars of the Roses.

As understood in the later-sixteenth century the Wars of the Roses encompassed 86 years of English history: what happened between the summer of 1399 and the summer of 1485. The key event was the deposition of a lawful king. The consequences were a divine punishment on not just the royal family but also the whole of England. Hall, in his preface, drew a clear distinction between normal division caused by faction and controversy, which he admitted unfortunately still existed, and the unnatural dynastic division between Lancaster and York which had infested England: a division the consequence of which, he claimed, 'my wit cannot comprehend nor my tongue declare neither yet my pen fully set forth'.[10] This indescribable hell on earth had by God's grace been set aside by the marriage of Henry VII and Elizabeth of York and, when he wrote, stood 'suspended and appalled' in the person of Henry VIII. Sir Thomas Smith was more willing to attempt a description of hell. 'By reason of titles', he stressed, 'this poor realm had never long rest'. The curse destroyed the royal family. 'And when this fell upon the head', he asked, 'how sped the body think you? . . . Blood pursued blood and ensued blood till all the realm was brought to great confusion . . . England in the latter end of King Henry VI was almost a very chaos. . . .'[11] In Smith's colourful account we can recognise some of his sources: rolls of parliament and early Tudor enclosure acts as well as the first histories. More significantly we should note how everything known about the fifteenth century – its economic difficulties as well as its political instability – has been subsumed under the one controlling idea of chaos.

This was the scenario taken up by Shakespeare. If one were to sit through all eight plays of the history cycle from Richard II to Richard III one would be periodically reminded that the theme and unity of the whole were the working out of divine retribution for the crime of deposing Richard II. The idea is there in the bishop of Carlisle's prediction in *Richard II*; in Henry V's prayer before Agincourt; and finally in Richmond's prayer of thanksgiving at the end of *Richard III*. But there is more to Shakespeare's cycle than a restatement of the conventional late-sixteenth-century interpretation of English history before 1485. There is a sense that the audience witnesses political behaviour common to all ages. It is both England then and England now. Implicit in the text is Hall's observation that all other divisions still flourish. In addition to a warning to contemporaries not to rebel against Elizabeth I, there may also be a debate about whether it is better to suffer tyranny or take the consequences of overthrowing it. Moreover on another plane the plays can be seen as a nostalgic lament for a lost paradise – a golden age associated with the era of Edward III when all was well in the political world.[12] By Shakespeare's day the idea of the Wars of the Roses had passed beyond mere propaganda: it was a perception of English history accepted as the truth on the basis of which it was possible to offer contemporary political debate and comment.

A second influence entered English historiography in the

sixteenth century: the Renaissance. Humanism was influential in two ways. It enhanced the status of history as a branch of literature. At first this meant classical, especially Roman, history. But following the pioneering work of Polydore Vergil and Sir Thomas More in the early decades of the sixteenth century there was a conscious effort to develop a native history, a history of England written not in Latin but in the vernacular. Secondly the perception of English history before 1500 was coloured by the humanist outlook on learning. To the humanist there were only two ages worth considering: the ancient and the modern in which good letters had been revived. Between the two lay the long, benighted Middle Ages. In extending this perception to England, humanists identified the accession of Henry VII in 1485 as the turning point. Soon it was taken for granted that England before 1485 was medieval and barbarous. The idea dovetailed neatly with the idea of the Wars of the Roses. Thus the wars were not only the anarchy from which Henry VII had rescued a suffering kingdom but also the final death throes of the Dark Ages; an idea caught beautifully in the nineteenth century by Bishop Stubbs: 'it was "as the morning spread upon the mountain", darkest before dawn'.[13]

The later evolution of the historical interpretation of the fifteenth century is inseparable from the development of history as an academic discipline. Until the late-nineteenth century the received wisdom, a marriage of Tudor propaganda and humanist prejudice, was irresistible. Admittedly an idiosyncratic unorthodoxy developed which took a provocatively favourable view of Richard III. Sir George Buck in the early-seventeenth century, Horace Walpole in the late-eighteenth century and Caroline Halsted in the early-nineteenth sought to reverse Henry VII's and Shakespeare's image. But this owed more to the personal temperaments of the authors than to a fundamental reappraisal of the subject.[14] The cumulative effect of the quickening antiquarian interest in the eighteenth and nineteenth centuries and the development of modern historical research in the nineteenth – the exploration and publication of government archives, legal records and private papers of the era – was to tend to confirm the received wisdom. The Paston Letters, first readily available in Fenn's edition (1787–1823), later supplemented by the publication of Smyth's *Lives of the Berkeleys* (1883–85) provided plenty of evidence of skulduggery in fifteenth-century East Anglia and Gloucestershire. Sir Harry Nicolas' six-volume *Proceedings of the Privy Council* in 1836 and the steady stream of publication by the Deputy Keeper of Public Records, the Rolls series and the Camden Society brought more and more contemporary evidence to light which appeared to confirm all that was previously known. The records of King's Bench, more prolific for the fifteenth century than earlier, provided (and still provide) a further rich seam of evidence of lawlessness and disorder. The landscape revealed to the greatest of the first generation of modern historians of medieval England, Bishop William Stubbs, was anything but sublime. In the third volume of his *Constitutional History*, first published in 1878, confident in 'the power of good' to triumph in 'the progress of this world', he concluded:

> The most enthusiastic admirer of medieval life must grant that all that was good and great in it was languishing even to death; and the firmest believer in progress must admit that as yet there were few signs of returning health. The sun of the Plantagenets went down in clouds and thick darkness: the coming of the Tudors gave as yet no promise of light.[15]

Charles Plummer in his sketch of the Lancastrian and Yorkist period which introduced his edition of Sir John Fortescue's *The Governance of England* (1885) especially emphasised 'the overgrown power and insubordination of the nobles', the utter lawlessness of the aristocracy, as a canker of the times. He traced the origin of the evil, which he christened bastard feudalism, back to the days of Edward III and asserted that it reached its greatest height during the Lancastrian period. Backed by bands of armed men the great lords corrupted and perverted the law, overawed parliament and Crown, and prosecuted their own private wars without restraint. Ultimately the anarchy so created overwhelmed the realm.[16]

But it was William Denton, Fellow of Worcester College, who in 1888 delivered the most scathing denunciation of the fifteenth century and the Wars of the Roses. His account reads like a modernisation of Sir Thomas Smith's sketch three centuries earlier. From the deposition of Richard II the house of Lancaster and York turned on one another. Not only did they destroy each other, 'the baronage of England was almost extirpated'. 'The slaughter of the people was greater than in any former war on English soil', but 'want, exposure and disease carried off more than the most murderous weapons of war'. The commerce of England was almost destroyed; hamlets and villages disappeared, all the towns, save London, were well-nigh ruined;

> and this ruin was but a type of a deeper ruin. . . . The standard of morality could not well have been lower than it was at the end of the fifteenth century. Lust, cruelty and dishonesty were paraded before the eyes of the people.[17]

The principal cause lay not in a crime against God but in the degeneracy of an ill-educated and corrupt baronage. Indeed in one splendid passage Denton went so far as to suggest that the moral degeneration was matched by physical deterioration ('low in stature and feeble in frame') induced by the practice of teenage sexual intercourse (at fourteen or earlier).[18] Altogether the late-medieval baronage suffered from a most shocking want of muscular Christianity.

It was however during the nineteenth century that the application of the term Wars of the Roses was narrowed to the 30 years 1455–85. While the fifteenth century as a whole was shameful, the Wars of the Roses came to describe the nadir only. The new usage was summed up by the 1911 edition of the *Encyclopaedia Britannica* 'a name given to a series of civil wars in England during the reign of Henry VI, Edward IV and Richard III . . . matched by a ferocity and brutality which are practically unknown in the history of English wars before and since'.[19] Thus the backsliding era of the Wars of the Roses received short-shrift at the hands of eminent Victorians convinced of the progressive virtues of their own age.

Dissenting voices were, however, already being raised. In 1874, before Stubbs published his *Constitutional History*, J. R. Green in his controversial *Short History of the English People*, while acknowledging that 'there are few periods in our annals from which we turn with such weariness and disgust as from the Wars of the Roses', suggested that the savage and brutal strife was limited to great lords and their retainers. 'For the most part the trading and agricultural classes stood wholly apart.' While the baronage was dashing itself to pieces in battle after battle, the country at large enjoyed a general tranquillity.[20] His brief observations were followed up ten years later by Thorold Rogers whose study of wages and prices led him to declare that the agricultural class, 'must have had only a transient and languid interest in the faction fight which was going on around them' and, far from being impoverished, enjoyed a golden age of comparative prosperity.[21] These views were taken further a generation later by C. L. Kingsford, whose seminal Ford Lectures of 1923 *Prejudice and Promise in Fifteenth Century England* were the first attempt to counter the prejudice of succeeding generations and to draw attention to the promising features of fifteenth-century life. Drawing particularly on the Stonor letters and papers and the legal records in which he had immersed himself, he argued that the disruptive effect of the Wars of the Roses had been exaggerated and that neither civil disorder nor civil war necessarily affected the lives of the county gentry any more than it did ordinary men and women.[22]

The revisionist torch was passed to K. B. McFarlane who in the year in which Kingsford's Ford Lectures were published took his Final Schools at Oxford. Over a lifetime McFarlane gradually and painstakingly refined his views on the fifteenth-century nobility: in effect a continuing commentary on Plummer. In essence his argument was that the later Middle Ages were not uniquely or structurally corrupt or lawless. 'Bastard Feudalism' had its roots long before Edward III and continued to flourish long after the death of Henry VII. It was no more than a form of the clientage and patronage which had oiled the wheels of society throughout England's pre-industrialised history.[23] McFarlane did not publish directly on the subject of the Wars of the Roses until the year before his death. But by his teaching he inspired a generation of scholars to question more thoroughly received interpretations and explore more deeply the sources of fifteenth-century history. The result was that after 1960 there was an explosion of new writings on the wars. McFarlane himself was characteristically cautious, suggesting that the scale and impact of the wars were limited and that the onset of 'real warfare' was agonisingly slow because desired by no-one. The fundamental cause, he argued, lay not in the degeneration or overweening might of the nobility but on the contrary on the undermighty shoulders of Henry VI and the feebleness of central government. Lords and gentry tried to avoid committing themselves, putting a higher premium on survival than loyalty to one house or another, or indeed one magnate or another. Few noble lines were exterminated by the wars: if there were any lasting effect it was that the baronage was demoralised by three decades of political upheaval and uncertainty.[24]

McFarlane's views were in part echoed by J. R. Lander who also published a work on the Wars of the Roses in 1965. In a later summary of his views which appeared in 1976 Lander concluded that the Wars of the Roses were very limited in scale and effect; that there was little devastation, little looting, few sieges; and that the wars had only the most temporary effects on trade, and little on agriculture.[25] In the same year, Charles Ross stressed the same points. The wars had little impact on society:

> England in the later-fifteenth century was in fact the home of a rich, varied and vigorous civilization. To study it is to remain largely unaware that it was a product of an age of political violence, which did nothing to hinder its steady development.[26]

The same theme was taken up and emphasised even more by John Gillingham who stressed in 1981 that England in the age of the Wars of the Roses was 'a society organized for peace' and 'the most peaceful country in Europe'.[27] All that was wanting was S. B. Chrimes' declaration that the Wars of the Roses never took place at all.

Those who have wished to reverse the Victorian view of later-fifteenth-century society have not had it all their own way. Lander and Ross themselves both stressed the high level of violence which was endemic in late-medieval society. And although Ross conceded that the wars might have made matters worse, it was only in the work of R. L. Storey on their origins (endorsed by M. H. Keen in 1973) that a causal connection between aristocratic violence, lawlessness and the wars was sustained.[28] Following Storey, D. M. Loades re-emphasised in 1974 the chaos of factional quarrels among 'noble bandits', whose innumerable savage affrays justifiably led contemporaries to consider the 1450s and 1460s as a period of unprecedented disorder.[29] And Anthony Goodman in *The Wars of the Roses* (1981), pictured the wars as a long series of calamities, warning that the dearth of evidence concerning disruption and destruction should not necessarily be taken to mean that they did not occur.[30]

Like would-be Lancastrians and Yorkists themselves, historians in the last quarter of the twentieth century are divided over the scale, character and impact of the Wars of the Roses. Nevertheless a consensus has been reached on several issues. Whether the phrase 'the Wars of the Roses' is considered to be strictly appropriate or not, it is accepted that it describes three or four decades of political instability and periodic open civil war in the second half of the fifteenth century. Secondly it is accepted that one cannot describe the combatants as being irrevocably divided into two parties called Lancastrians and Yorkists; allegiances and alliances were considerably too fluid to enable one to allocate individual lords and gentlemen to one or other side throughout the period. Thirdly none but the most fervent admirer of the Tudors would argue that the later-fifteenth century was an era of moral delinquency or a time to be unsympathetically pitied. Fourthly discussion of the Wars of the Roses is now concentrated on interpreting political history, not on the moral or physical condition of society at large or its economic, ecclesiastical or cultural history. And finally, although narrower points of definition are debated as to precisely when the Wars should be said to have begun or ended, none would now argue that 1485 marked a clear break between one era and another, let alone 'The End of the Middle Ages'. On the whole the years 1450–1530 are perceived to have a unity. If 'modern' England is to be said to have a beginning at any particular time then that time is more likely to have been during the 1530s. If the 80 years before the break with Rome is to have any particular overall characteristic it lies in that overworked phrase 'an age of transition'.

Debate nevertheless continues about several aspects of the subject if only because of the quality of the evidence available to the historian. There can be no doubt that our detailed knowledge of this era is immeasurably greater than it was a century ago. While reconsideration of the concept of the Wars of the Roses is relatively recent, detailed historical research since 1900 has added greatly to the sheer quantity of information available. A line of monumental political studies from Cora Scofield's *Edward IV* (1924) to R. A. Griffiths' *The Reign of King Henry VI* (1981) stand witness to generations of painstaking search through the public records. The development of prosopographical studies, most particularly in the field of parliamentary history by J. C. Wedgwood and J. S. Roskell, has since the 1930s brought forward, and continues to reveal, more and more detail concerning the lives and careers of individual protagonists.[31] Since 1960 the dramatic expansion of British higher education and the realisation that the fifteenth century offered a relatively unworked field has quickened the pace of this research. Although in 1976 J. R. Lander drew attention to the enormous quantities of neglected archives, both government records and private papers, which were still awaiting students willing to plough through them, both before and since an unprecedented number of researchers have been at work. At first, in the postwar years, research concentrated on administrative, financial and constitutional topics. Then it turned to the as-yet untapped private collections, many newly deposited in county record offices, to study baronial families and, latterly, the gentry and county societies. The Beauforts, Courtenays, Greys of Ruthin, Howards, Mowbrays, Percies, Staffords, Stanleys, Tudors and Talbots all found their historian. Derbyshire, Devon, Herefordshire, Kent, Nottinghamshire, Staffordshire, Warwickshire and the West Riding of Yorkshire have all been, or currently are, the subject of doctoral theses. Anyone seeking to master all facets of fifteenth-century political life has to assimilate an ever-growing mass of detailed evidence.

While in sheer quantity of information more and more is made available, the principal lines of interpretation and issues of debate remain very much the same. Perhaps the most important change brought about by recent research has been the growing awareness of regional and local variation and the need for even greater care in making generalisations. What was true of Warwickshire may not have been true of North Yorkshire or Kent. Yet the evidence remains, as it always has been, incomplete and unreliable. Narrative accounts (the chronicles) are all to a lesser or greater degree partisan and imperfectly informed. The records of government, private individuals and corporations (mostly legal and financial documents) have the advantage of normally being politically neutral, but they yield mainly trivial information which is only cumulatively of value, and are exceptionally fragmented and frustratingly incomplete. Matters are made worse by the fact that many private collections dry up in the mid-fifteenth century. In J. R. Lander's memorable words; 'In reality the political history of the period is a web of shreds and tatters, patched up from meagre chronicles and from a few collections of letters in which exaggerated gossip and wild rumours have been, all too often, confused with facts'.[32] Whatever individual researchers may unearth from record sources, it is likely that the Wars of the Roses will remain one of the more inadequately documented and controversial topics of English political history.

Typical, and a matter for immediate consideration, is the failure to agree on how many Wars of the Roses there were, when each one started, when each ended and what distinguished one from another. Although Goodman characterised them as merely a series of upheavals between 1452 and 1497, most recent historians have opted for three wars of varying lengths. McFarlane suggested 1450–64; 1464–71; 1483–87: Gillingham concluded 1455–64; 1469–71; 1483–87: Ross gave 1460–64; 1469–71; 1483–87. But Ross also pointed out that in terms of dynastic struggle between Lancaster and York there were only two wars which ended in 1471.[33] This line is taken a step further here. Although there were indeed two distinct periods of open warfare with a lull between 1464 and 1469, the issues involved and the fundamental causes remained essentially the same between 1459 and 1471. In short, the wars of 1459–64 and 1469–71 were two stages of the same struggle: the wars of Lancaster and York. On the other hand the wars of 1483–87 were separate in cause, and different in issue: they were wars between York and Tudor. The story and analysis of the Wars of the Roses which follows is thus founded on the interpretation that there were in essence two wars: the first ending in 1471, the second beginning in 1483. It will be noted too that recent historians have dated the outbreak of the first of these two wars variously between 1450 and 1460: there is no longer a consensus concerning 1455. In this study 1459 is taken as the beginning of the first Wars of the Roses. While it is certainly the case that the first battle of St Albans in 1455 was a major civil disturbance, it was an isolated clash, part of a long prelude to the sustained conflict which broke out four years later.

2

THE COURSE OF THE WARS

Prelude to the wars: 1450–59

In 1450 England's king was Henry VI, a young man in his late twenties.[1] He was the son of the famous warrior Henry V, a father he had not known for he came to the throne when he was nine months old. He had no memory of being other than king. He had been cossetted and nurtured to step into his father's martial shoes. He had inherited two kingdoms, being crowned king of England in 1429 and king of France in 1431. From the age of sixteen in 1437 he had begun to play an active part in the affairs of the kingdom. By 1439 his minority was at an end. It had been a surprisingly harmonious minority. Rifts, conflicts and factional rivalry had, of course, occurred, but the leading councillors and nobles, inspired by their dedication to the memory of Henry V whom they had served, had been at one in their determination to hand on to his young heir his inheritance in both kingdoms.

Henry VI was, however, almost the complete opposite of his father. Where Henry V had been the paragon of chivalry, Henry VI eschewed the field of battle. In 1440 when all seemed propitious for him to lead his subjects to war in defence of his father's conquests, he turned instead to the foundation of Eton College.[2] The war in France was henceforth left to his leading subjects. In England he rapidly fell under the domination of an unscrupulous court faction. After 10 years of personal rule, before his 30th birthday, Henry was faced with the greatest political crisis since the reign of Richard II. Following years of indecision and duplicity, Normandy was lost to France with scarcely a blow given in one of the most ignominious campaigns ever conducted by an English army (1449–50). At the height of the crisis parliamentary anger and popular rebellion shook Henry's regime to its foundations. His principal adviser, William de la Pole, duke of Suffolk was impeached, sent into exile, intercepted and murdered.

The year 1450 provided the opportunity for Richard of York, Henry's greatest subject and heir presumptive (for although Henry had married Margaret of Anjou in 1445 he still had no children) to bid for political power. York had been excluded in the previous decade. Removed from the command in Normandy, in 1447 he had been sent off as lieutenant of Ireland. Untainted by the failure of recent policy he returned to England determined to establish himself as the king's chief minister. He found, however, that the king had turned to none other than Edmund Beaufort, duke of Somerset, the last and discredited governor of Normandy. Try as he might, York and his allies could not impose themselves on the king. In 1452, having spent a period in voluntary internal exile in his marcher Welsh lordships, York raised an army and sought to force his way into office. At Dartford his army was outfaced by the forces of the court. York submitted and he was allowed to return once more to self-imposed exile.

After York's defeat at Dartford, Somerset and his friends were able to tighten their grip on power. In fact there are signs that in these years after the fall of Suffolk Henry VI himself was beginning to play a more decisive role in affairs. He showed greater vigour in suppressing the popular rebellion of 1450, he began to show himself more to his subjects and when in 1452, in answer to an appeal from a group of dissident Gascons, the veteran earl of Shrewsbury was able to recover Bordeaux and much of Gascony (Gascony had been overrun by the French in 1451) he was able to rally considerable support for his regime. By the summer of 1453 it was beginning to look as though Henry VI's reign was set on a new and more steady course.

In August 1453 two, possibly connected, events occurred which decisively changed the situation. First Henry heard that Shrewsbury had been defeated and killed at Castillon; secondly, a few days later, he collapsed into a state of what has been identified as catatonic schizophrenia: total mental withdrawal from the world. For fifteen months or more Henry did not, could not or would not communicate with a single living soul (later it was to be imagined that he was communicating exclusively with God). This sudden, unexpected, event, for Henry had never previously shown signs of mental instability whatever other shortcomings he may have had, threw the political world into new turmoil.

After several months of uncertainty, and with no sign of recovery, in March 1454 a protectorate was established. Henry's condition was comparable to childhood and the precedent for a minority was to place the government of the kingdom into the hands of a protector and council. Precedent also determined that the protector should be the senior adult male member of the royal family: in 1454 this was Richard of York. And so in circumstances entirely unpredictable and after four years of apparent failure, York achieved his ambition and more. York's position as protector was strengthened by the recruitment of powerful new allies: the Nevilles father and son, who were the earls of Salisbury and Warwick. But the Nevilles had become embroiled in a private war in Yorkshire with the earl of Northumberland and the price of their support was the protector's backing, given under the guise of royal pacification, in securing a victory over their rival. Warwick too was in dispute with the duke of Somerset in south Wales. Somerset found himself not only dismissed, but also committed to the Tower. In the midst of this Queen Margaret gave birth to a son, Edward. York was no longer heir presumptive and had measurably less cause in future to claim that he should be high in the king's council.

The process of polarisation which took place in 1454 was only hastened by the king's recovery early in 1455. Soon Somerset was released. If not before, he now found that he had a powerful ally in the person of Queen Margaret whose son's interests had to be defended. York and the Nevilles withdrew from court. In May rival armies met at St Albans. In a brief skirmish which took place in the king's presence, Somerset, the earl of Northumberland and one of his sons were hacked to death. The king was escorted back to Westminster with his old advisers. Whether because he had been wounded or because he suffered a second mental collapse, Henry once more became incapacitated and the protectorate was restored. But a new and deadly element had now been introduced. Blood had been shed. What had been rivalry for place had been transformed into feud. The new duke of Somerset sought revenge for the death of his father, Edmund; the new earl of Northumberland sought revenge for the death of his. The young heirs allied themselves with Margaret of Anjou who clearly emerged at this point as the new leader of the court faction. York was removed from his second protectorate early in 1456 although he continued to act as chief minister for several months. But in the autumn of the same year his friends were removed from office and replaced by men more inclined to the queen. The king was by now no more than a figurehead. His health would seem to have been permanently damaged. And although there is no evidence of a return to his condition of 1453–55, there can be little doubt that eventually he became nothing but the pathetic puppet of faction.

These years are perhaps the most obscure in the whole of the fifteenth century. It is possible that before 1458 the hotheads, perhaps even the queen herself, were held at bay by a group under the duke of Buckingham who still sought, ineffectively, to find some means of reconciliation. York and his friends were not totally excluded. In March 1458 a grandiose 'Loveday' (ritual reconciliation) was staged, at which the sons of the victims of St Albans and the victors publicly made reconciliation and agreed terms of restitution. It proved to be an empty charade but the effort made and the king's own shadowy role in the proceedings suggest that as yet the point of no return had not been reached. It would seem that the principals were only too conscious of the potential dangers and were desperately seeking to avert a revival of overt conflict which would only be more catastrophic.

That moment came one step nearer in the autumn of 1458. A

brawl broke out at court from which the earl of Warwick had to fight his way clear. There may even have been an attempted assassination. He promptly withdrew to Calais of which he was captain and where he had the backing of a strong garrison. Immediately following, the chief officers of state were changed and men more closely associated with the queen took over.[3] During 1459 the queen, now unequivocally in control, began to take steps to deal with York and the Nevilles once and for all. Plans were laid to condemn the Yorkists for treason at a council meeting in the summer and preparations were begun to enforce such a decision by arms. The Yorkist lords knowing fully what was in store, themselves took up arms. While the Court gathered its strength in the midlands, based at Coventry, the Yorkist lords planned to gather at Worcester in September. Warwick came over from Calais, while Salisbury marched down from north Yorkshire to meet York at Ludlow before moving up to Worcester. Salisbury was intercepted by royal troops at Blore Heath in Staffordshire, but was able to defeat the army led by Lord Audley and press on, if somewhat reduced in numbers, to the rendezvous. At Worcester the three lords declared their continuing loyalty to the king but their determination to rid him of his evil ministers. Pressed by a superior royal army they retreated to Ludlow and there, before the town, at Ludford drew up the army for battle. But on the night of 12/13 October, knowing that they were heavily outnumbered and discovering desertion by key elements of the Calais garrison which had accompanied Warwick, the lords decamped and fled; York making his way to Ireland, Warwick and Salisbury to Calais.

The first wars: 1459–71

If one is to pick any moment when open civil war began it would be the campaign of 1459. It came after several years of political deterioration and several months of military preparation. It was intended by both sides to be a decisive test of strength in which no mercy was to have been shown to the losers. The battle lines had been clearly drawn. As yet the objective was still domination of the court and removal of all rivals. The queen enjoyed overwhelming numerical support among the English nobility and gentry. All but a handful of the peerage rallied to her cause. The appeal of loyalty to the king was still strong. York and his allies were too easily cast in the role of malcontents. But the Yorkist lords, though heavily outnumbered, had compensatory material and military strength. They were three of the richest and most powerful magnates. Not only could York tap the resources of his Welsh marcher lordships, but Warwick commanded the Calais garrison and Salisbury could draw on the military experience and strength of the far north. Militarily the two sides were not as ill-matched as a roll call of peers would suggest.

In October 1459 Queen Margaret completed her design of proscribing her enemies. At a pliant parliament called to meet at Coventry (the parliament of Devils), York and his followers were found guilty of treason by attainders and their lands forfeited and occupied by royal officers or distributed to loyal supporters. The Yorkists had no other option but force to reverse these acts. For the time being they were safe in Dublin and Calais. But the Court lost no time in trying to recover Calais. The duke of Somerset was appointed captain and early in 1460 began a siege of the town. Its defence was under the direction of Salisbury's brother, William, Lord Fauconberg, an immensely experienced veteran of the Hundred Years' War. Warwick and Salisbury were able to slip out of Calais and to sail to Dublin to coordinate plans with the duke. After their return, in June, they launched an invasion of south-eastern England. Marching via London, where a royal garrison was left bottled up in the Tower, Warwick and the earl of March (York's eldest son and the future Edward IV) came up against the king's army at Northampton. There, thanks to the timely switch to the Yorkist side by Lord Grey of Ruthin, the royal army was defeated and its leaders – the duke of Buckingham, the earl of Shrewsbury and Lord Beaumont – killed, while the king fell into Yorkist hands. Returning in triumph to London the lords installed themselves in office and at court and sent out writs summoning a parliament to Westminster in October, the principal intended business being the reversal of the attainders passed in 1459.

York himself delayed, or was delayed, in returning to England. When he did land he immediately caused a stir by displaying the royal banner and marching up to London in the manner of king. Timing his arrival to coincide with the gathering of parliament he strode purposefully into Westminster Hall and laid his hand on the throne. Thus for the first time did York declare his dynastic ambition. His act was not met by acclaim. According to one or two reports it even surprised his closest associates. Doubt has recently been raised about this, but the clear truth seems to have been that not even this parliament, called when the Yorkists were fully in control, would accede to the deposition of Henry VI.[4] Ultimately a quite unworkable compromise was patched up: Henry was to keep the throne for his lifetime; York was declared his heir in place of his seven-year-old son.

It was one thing to pass such an act; it was quite another to enforce it. Queen Margaret with her son was at large gathering troops in the west country, Wales and the north even before the November 'Accord' was reached. They now had even greater cause to reverse the decision of Northampton. York and his followers too faced an urgent need to suppress her and to recover control of their estates. Thus after parliament went down, York and Salisbury set out in strength for the north, there to confront the queen. They reached Sandal, York's castle near Wakefield, but on the last day of the year were caught foraging. York and his son the earl of Rutland were killed on the field; Salisbury shortly after. Among the victorious Lancastrian leaders were the duke of Somerset and the earl of Northumberland. St Albans had been avenged. The earl of March, now duke of York, in the meantime had set off to Wales to attempt to gain control there. On 2 February 1461, at Mortimer's Cross, he defeated the earl of Pembroke and secured that front. However, Queen Margaret was already pushing south with an army whose size and lack of discipline spread terror as it passed. On 17 February, at St Albans, it met and defeated Warwick who had marched out from London to face it. With Henry VI back in her hands the capital now lay at the queen's mercy. But she failed to press home her advantage. As she hesitated, she heard that March, having met with the fleeing Warwick, was now on his way up to challenge her. Faced with this new threat the queen withdrew leaving March to enter London unopposed on 27 February. Five days later, declaring that Henry VI had forfeited his right to the throne by failing to honour the November Accord, Edward IV took possession of the throne. Barely hesitating to raise reinforcements, Edward IV set out once more in pursuit of the queen's army that had retreated north. Catching up with the Lancastrians in southern Yorkshire the decisive engagement which had been threatened since October 1459 finally took place on the field of Towton. After a long and bloody battle, Edward IV emerged victorious. Henry VI, Queen Margaret and Prince Edward, who had been behind the lines in York, escaped to Scotland. Edward IV returned in triumph to London to be crowned.

Henry VI's reign may well have come to an end, but civil war was not over. Lancastrians held strongholds in the far north of England and Wales. Their king and his heir were still at large. Edward IV could not feel completely secure on the throne until all pockets of Lancastrian resistance were crushed and his Lancastrian rivals killed. It was to take him ten years and considerable upheaval to achieve both these ends. Relying on Scottish and French support Queen Margaret was at first hopeful of an early comeback. Several Lancastrian plots were unearthed in the first years of the reign; disturbances occurred in several parts of the kingdom; and there were frequent invasion scares in southern England. In Wales the castle of Harlech was garrisoned by Lancastrians until 1468. Far more dangerously, operating from a safe refuge north of the border Lancastrians were for three years after 1461 a constant threat to Northumberland. The castles of Alnwick, Bamburgh and Dunstanburgh became the focal point of a long-drawn out battle for control. Twice Warwick and his brother John, Lord Montagu, took these castles (September 1461, December 1462). Twice the Lancastrians retook them (October 1462, March/May 1463). It was not until the spring and early summer of 1464 that Lancastrian threats to the far north were finally crushed. Following two victories won by Lord Montagu at Hedgeley

Moor and Hexham the Northumbrian castles were for a third and final time reduced. During all this time Henry VI and Prince Edward remained safely out of Edward's clutches. Henry VI seems to have divided his time between Scotland and Northumberland. Prince Edward was taken to France in 1463. After the final suppression of Northumberland Henry VI roamed as an exile in northern England sheltered by loyal servants. In July 1465 he was tracked down and captured. Lodged in the Tower, his life was spared because it would have been both pointless and counterproductive to have killed him. Killing Henry would only have passed the Lancastrian torch to Prince Edward in France; and such a needless death would have been a propaganda gift to his enemies. Henry thus languished a prisoner in the Tower.

After 1465 Edward could perhaps have begun to look forward to more secure and relaxed times. However the clouds of war began to blow up again from another direction. In May 1464, while ostensibly marching north to pacify Northumberland, Edward IV secretly married Elizabeth Woodville at Stony Stratford. The marriage undertaken at a time when Warwick was in good faith conducting negotiations with France for the king's hand naturally piqued the earl. But he put on a good face and publicly showed no opposition. The king's marriage was bound, however, to have wider implications, particularly as the new queen came from a prolific English family, had been married before and had several Lancastrian connections. Regardless of the question of etiquette involved in the king's marriage to a widow of not quite the right birth, it set up political repercussions. Historians have been divided as to the extent to which the Woodvilles, as the queen's relations and friends are conveniently called, were inordinately favoured. They may not have received excessive grants of land, but in one respect, by cornering the upper reaches of the marriage market, they had an important bearing on future developments.[5] Moreover the queen, any queen, was likely to set up a separate and alternative political focal point. It may not have been entirely against Edward's will that a group known afterwards as the New Yorkists, focusing on the queen's father Earl Rivers, and Lord Herbert, earl of Pembroke emerged at court to counterbalance the enormous power and influence of the Nevilles. Whatever the precise cause, and it may be no more than a working out of an inevitable rift between a king determined to be the master of his own house and a kingmaker naturally reluctant to see his prominent position whittled away, relationships between Warwick and his king began to cool and worsen. The turning point was almost certainly a difference over the policy to be adopted towards France and the Netherlands where the king of France and the duke of Burgundy were intense rivals. Warwick had come to favour a pro-French line; the king, supported by the queen (her mother was of the house of Luxembourg in the Netherlands) and her friends, came to prefer a Burgundian alliance. In 1468 Edward completed an agreement for the marriage of his sister Margaret with Charles the Bold, the new duke of Burgundy. Insult was added to injury by the manner in which he allowed the earl to conduct futile negotiations for an alternative match while the Burgundian alliance was also being pursued. Although Warwick still came occasionally to Court, by the end of 1468 his hostility to the queen and her family and his estrangement from the king were being noticed. Towards the end of 1468 serious Lancastrian plots were uncovered. There was, moreover, growing popular disillusion with the new government. In these circumstances the breach between Edward IV and Warwick burst into open conflict in the summer of 1469.

Over the next two years, 1469–71, there was reenacted the same sequence of events as had occurred in the 1450s. A disgruntled mighty subject at first tried to force himself back into influence at Court and then, failing that, sought to depose the king. The action moved more rapidly and more bewilderingly partly because the understudies of the 1450s were now the leading players; partly because both principals had been on the stage before; and partly because the alternative king was waiting in the wings. Warwick laid his plans well. In July 1469 he slipped across to Calais to celebrate the marriage of his elder daughter, Isabel, with the king's twenty-year-old brother, George, duke of Clarence. This marriage had earlier been vetoed by the king, who nevertheless, by his backing of ambitious Woodville marriages, had virtually left the earl no alternative for befitting

29

husbands for his two daughters and heiresses other than members of the royal family. Clarence, who was to prove himself an ambitious but weak, vacillating and untrustworthy man had clearly been suborned by the earl. The Calais marriage was in effect a declaration of opposition. At the same time the latest of a series of northern risings led by 'Robin of Redesdale' revealed itself to be a rising of Warwick's substantial northern affinity under the leadership of a member of the Conyers family, stalwart and long-serving retainers of the Nevilles. Their force marched south and having united with Warwick and Clarence came up against a royal army at Edgecote near Banbury. At this engagement, largely due to dissension in their ranks, the king's men were overwhelmed and afterwards Earl Rivers, and the earls of Pembroke and Devon were executed. Three days later Warwick took the king prisoner. For two months at the most Warwick sought to rule in the king's name, keeping the king himself under arrest first in Warwick, then at Middleham in north Yorkshire. But a Lancastrian rising by Warwick's kinsman, Sir Humphrey Neville, which threatened Warwick as much as the king, could only be suppressed if the king were at large. Consequently early in September he was released. Like York before him Warwick had discovered that it was impossible to rule through a captive king, especially a king in the prime of life.

Edward IV seems for the time being neither to have had the strength nor the inclination to seek retribution against Warwick and his brother. They were welcomed at Court, although the king began to take steps to guard against a repetition. When six months later Warwick and Clarence rose again, Edward IV was ready to take swift and decisive action. The earl and duke took advantage of a feud in Lincolnshire to foster a new rising in March 1470. But the king moved promptly and dispersed the rebel force at the ironically named Losecoat Field near Stamford. No sooner had this been accomplished than he heard news that Warwick was raising north Yorkshire and Clarence the west country in a plan to put Clarence himself on the throne. Pressing north, and in strength, Edward secured Yorkshire before turning south in pursuit of Warwick and Clarence who fled to Devon and took ship at Dartmouth for France. Warwick was totally discredited.

There now followed the most dramatic volte-face in the whole history of these wars. In France Warwick was induced on 22 July to perform a solemn and public reconciliation with Queen Margaret which was sealed by a marriage the following month between Warwick's younger daughter Anne and Prince Edward. Thus once more Warwick became a loyal servant of the house of Lancaster, committed to the restoration of Henry VI. No time was lost mounting, with French help, an invasion of England. Edward IV took full precautions for coastal defence, but Warwick outmanoeuvred him by calling upon his northern retainers to rise once more. In August Edward had no choice but to march north to crush this, the third rebellion of northerners against him in twelve months. He knew all too well how dangerous such a movement could be if left unchecked. The rebellion melted away in front of him and the leaders submitted. But they had done their work.[6] While Edward was still in Yorkshire, Warwick landed in the west country. Learning that many English nobles had declared for Warwick in the name of Henry VI and discovering that Warwick's brother Montagu had also gone over, Edward, with only his household and a remnant of loyal noblemen with him, realised that he had been outmanoeuvred and isolated. Now himself taking flight he found ships at Kings Lynn and escaped to the Netherlands and the protection of his brother-in-law Charles, duke of Burgundy.

Thus on 3 October 1470 Henry VI was restored to the throne, the Readeption as contemporary legal documents put it. A broken 50-year-old, he could only have been a caretaker monarch until his son, by all accounts a young man of his grandfather's chivalric mettle, was ready to take his place. The return of the queen and the prince was, however, fatefully delayed both by the queen's excessive caution and, latterly, adverse winds. When the Lancastrian party did finally land in England in April it was too late. The wheel of fortune had turned once more. For Edward IV, aided by Burgundy, who was faced by a Franco-Lancastrian alliance, had already returned to recover his kingdom.

Edward IV's recovery of the throne in March–May 1471 was

a remarkable feat of arms, achieved, as his own official and chivalrically inspired account willingly admitted, against all the odds. He landed at Ravenspur in Holderness accompanied by only a few men – his brother Richard, duke of Gloucester, Anthony Woodville, the new Earl Rivers and William, Lord Hastings included. Claiming, as Henry IV had before him, that he was returning solely to recover his duchy, he was admitted reluctantly to the city of York. He moved west to his lordship of Wakefield where he had hoped to raise troops but found little enthusiasm. Yet he was able to leave Yorkshire unmolested partly because of the studied neutrality of Henry Percy, earl of Northumberland, whom a year earlier he had restored, and partly because of the inability of Lord Montagu to raise troops to resist him. In the midlands he received much needed support from followers of Lord Hastings. Pressing on towards Coventry he sought an engagement with the earl of Warwick. The decisive moment occurred when his brother George, duke of Clarence, at the head of a force raised in the south-west threw in his lot with Edward. The Yorkists, unable to force Warwick into battle, then marched up to London which opened its gates. Warwick had followed and finally the two armies came to blows in thick fog at Barnet on Easter Sunday, 14 April. In a more than usually confused battle Edward was victorious: Warwick and Montagu lay dead on the field.

There was, however, no time for the victor to rest for Edward received news of the landing at Weymouth of Queen Margaret, Prince Edward and an army. The Lancastrians, having heard of Warwick's defeat, sought to reach the comparative safety of Wales. But Edward, after a forced march, intercepted them at Tewkesbury before they could cross the Severn. And there on 4 May the Lancastrians too were defeated, the duke of Somerset, the earl of Devon and, most significantly, Prince Edward being killed either in the field or shortly afterwards. Secondary risings in the north and Kent having been suppressed, Edward was able to return in triumph to London on 21 May. On the self same night Henry VI was put to death, almost certainly on the orders of Edward IV himself. Edward IV had recovered his throne through a combination of his own boldness and decisiveness, his enemies' indecision and a generous slice of luck.

The first wars ended on the night that Henry VI was murdered. Since the moment Richard of York publicly advanced his claim to the throne in the autumn of 1460 there had been two rival dynasties claiming to rule England. There had been open warfare from 1459 to 1464, if only sporadically after Towton in March 1461. It had resurfaced again in 1469. Throughout the first reign of Edward IV, while Prince Edward remained at large in France, the potential of renewed dynastic conflict, realised in 1470, had always existed. Only after his death, and in its wake, that of the unfortunate Henry VI, was this threat removed. It took the Yorkists ten and a half years to destroy the Lancastrian dynasty.

The second wars: 1483–87

After 1471 Edward IV was secure on the throne. By all reasonable prediction the Wars of the Roses, the wars between Lancaster and York, should have been over. Yet they were not. In 1483, on the death of Edward IV, England was plunged once more into turmoil. There had been few indications that this would be the case. Admittedly it had taken Edward IV two more years fully to suppress all opposition. In 1473 there were landings in both the south-west and north-east by die-hard Lancastrians, but thereafter there were no further signs of Lancastrian resistance or rebellion. Nor is this surprising. After the death of the childless Prince Edward, the only remaining claimants to the Lancastrian title were either distant geographically, in the person of King John II of Portugal, or feeble dynastically (through the female Beaufort line), in the person of Henry Tudor, earl of Richmond. Only a tiny rump of die-hards, including the earl of Oxford, Lord Clifford and the claimant to the earldom of Devon besides Henry Tudor's uncle Jasper, earl of Pembroke, clung to his remote chance of succession. Mainstream opinion concluded that rightly or wrongly, the Yorkist dynasty was established. Many old Lancastrians who had opted for exile with Queen Margaret or stood out in rebellion in the 1460s now returned to

England and royal service, prominent among them being John Morton, who became bishop of Ely, Sir John Fortescue, the eminent lawyer and Sir Richard Tunstall. Edward IV did not totally dismiss the threat of Tudor as a pretender in exile in Brittany. From time to time, in a somewhat desultory manner, he sought to persuade the duke of Brittany to hand him over. By 1482, moreover, there were signs that, through the good offices of his mother, Margaret Beaufort, now married to Thomas, Lord Stanley, Richmond was ready to reconcile himself with the Yorkist regime.[7]

After 1471 Edward IV ruled with firmness and authority, if not high-handedly. Until 1475 he was preoccupied with forming a triple alliance with Brittany and Burgundy in order to mount an invasion of France. It is not clear whether he was inspired to emulate the feats of Henry V or more pragmatically motivated by a desire to unite a divided realm against a common foe: to make outward war to secure inward peace. After the invasion ended ingloriously but profitably at Picquigny where Louis XI bought Edward off, the king seems to have had no further ambition save to enjoy his state. The only major event to ruffle the calm was the arrest, trial and death of the incorrigible duke of Clarence in 1477–78. Clarence may well not have been guilty of treason, but since 1470 he had never again been fully trusted by his brother and by his folly brought his judicial murder upon himself. From 1478 the king appeared to be presiding over a harmonious Court and country. In his last years a moderately successful war with Scotland was offset by a debacle in foreign policy which left him isolated and without the French pension paid since 1475. When he died, after a short illness at the early age of 42, the talking point was whether England would be drawn once more into a continental war.

Within three months of Edward IV's death, the kingdom had once more been thrown into confusion. The applecart was upset not by an exiled pretender, but by a member of the king's own family – Richard, duke of Gloucester. Gloucester was a man who had won universal respect for his probity and loyalty to his brother, as well as his piety, courage and chivalric zeal. His qualities stood out in stark contrast to his fickle and untrustworthy brother of Clarence. Nor was his high reputation without foundation. Having assumed the mantle of the earl of Warwick in northern England (he married his younger daughter Anne, widowed by the death of Prince Edward) he had with considerable skill both secured the loyalty of the region to the regime and brought a measure of good government and local concord which had not been known for two decades. The last person anyone expected to be a threat to the peaceful succession of the twelve-year-old Edward V was his paternal uncle Richard.

Events on Edward IV's death were to show that the harmony within the Yorkist court was more apparent than real. Resentments and feuds ran beneath the surface which only the king's imposing presence had been able to contain. Lord Hastings and the queen's son by her first marriage, Thomas Grey, marquis of Dorset were rivals. The queen herself seems to have resented Gloucester. A tense atmosphere as the major politicians manoeuvred for initial advantage during the new king's minority was quickly created. The queen sought to establish herself as regent. This was promptly stopped by the majority of the council which preferred to follow constitutional precedent and to accept Richard of Gloucester as protector. His office of protector would only have lasted until the king was crowned; as the king was twelve this could take place immediately. Thereafter the duke could have expected to preside over the council until the king, like Henry VI, could begin to exercise his own authority when he reached his sixteenth birthday in November 1487. While coming up to London three weeks after Edward IV's death, however, and before a council could formally agree to his role, the duke took matters into his own hands. At Stony Stratford at dawn on 30 April, with the assistance of a new-found ally, Henry, duke of Buckingham, he arrested Earl Rivers, Lord Richard Grey, the queen's younger son by her first marriage, and Thomas Vaughan, the chamberlain of the new king's household, and took forcible possession of the young king's person. By this *coup d'état* Gloucester secured the protectorate, but he also made an implacable enemy out of Earl Rivers and set himself on a course, which, if not already determined, led inexorably to taking the throne for himself.

First reactions to this *coup* revealed that the queen immediately feared that the lives of herself and her younger son were in danger, for she hurriedly retreated to sanctuary in Westminster Abbey. Gloucester was duly made protector and set in motion the arrangements for the coronation and the calling of the new king's first parliament. Neither event was to take place. In a frantic two weeks in the middle of June, Gloucester seized and executed without trial William, Lord Hastings, who had until that moment publicly supported him; arrested Lord Stanley and the two most influential clerical councillors, John Morton, bishop of Ely and Thomas Rotherham, archbishop of York; browbeat the queen mother to surrender herself and her younger son from sanctuary; cancelled the parliament; and on 22 June formally claimed the throne for himself on the grounds of the bastardy of Edward V and his brother. There was no resistance. 'Elected' by a body of London citizens and would-be members of parliament who had already come up to Westminster, he took the throne on 26 June. On 6 July, in solemn state, he was crowned.

It was, with the element of surprise on his side, comparatively easy for Richard III to take the throne. It was more difficult to hold. By his act he had split the Yorkist establishment in two. He had powerful and committed support in the north (which included the northern earls of Northumberland and Westmorland) and the duke of Buckingham on his side. He won over John, Lord Howard (by granting him his claim to the duchy of Norfolk), his nephew John de la Pole, earl of Lincoln and heir to the duchy of Suffolk and several lesser Yorkist peers. His base of support was not too narrow. But against him were ranged all those who had leant towards the Woodvilles and most of Edward IV's exhousehold men. Although taken off guard in June, these men regrouped and in late September raised most of the southern counties with the objective of restoring Edward V. The rising probably sealed the deposed king's fate, for it quickly became clear to the rebels that he and his brother were dead. In their place they turned to the exiled Henry Tudor who overnight found his prospects transformed. Henry sailed to England; but arrived to find the rising crushed and turned back to Brittany.

Henry, duke of Buckingham, in an almost inexplicable volte-face, threw in his lot with the rebels, was quickly captured and summarily executed. He had been liberally rewarded by Richard III and could hardly complain that he had been cold-shouldered. He might simply have misjudged the situation and believed he was joining the winning side. He might even have imagined that he had an opportunity to make himself king, for he too had a claim through his great grandmother, the daughter of Edward III's youngest son, Thomas of Woodstock. Buckingham's early defection was a shattering blow to Richard's confidence, probably more disheartening than the risings of disgruntled members of his brother's disbanded household and friends of the Woodvilles which he may well have half-expected.

After October 1483 Richard had fewer supporters on whom he could rely. Lord Stanley, because of his wife's proven complicity in the risings of the autumn of 1483, and despite his publicly displayed loyalty during the crisis, could not be fully trusted. The king fell back more overtly on the support of his trusted ducal following, predominantly northern in character, many of whom were given rewards and key offices in the dissident south. This no doubt solved a short-term problem of security, but the evident unpopularity of his 'plantation' only exacerbated his longer-term standing. A steady trickle of defections continued to his enemies abroad. Henry Tudor presented himself as a rallying point for old Yorkists by his solemn oath to marry Edward IV's eldest surviving child, Princess Elizabeth and rule jointly with her (the second part he did not fulfil). Richard III's morale was further damaged by the death of his only son and newly created Prince of Wales in the spring of 1484. At the same time he had to take the unusual step of issuing public statements reiterating his title to the throne and ordering the local authorities to quash false rumours about it. Richard wisely tried to rebuild his bridges with the queen dowager, Elizabeth Woodville, and won a minor victory when she agreed finally to leave sanctuary and, with her daughters, join the Court. Early in 1485, however, after the death of his queen, rumours quickly spread that he poisoned her. A growing desperation is indicated by his plan to marry Elizabeth of York himself, a scheme which would no doubt have scotched Henry Tudor. But this foundered on the rock of the intransigence of his principal councillors, especially Catesby and Ratcliffe, who well knew that such a marriage would have been accompanied by a general Woodville restoration and a loss of their own privileged position and hold on forfeited lands. The king was forced to take the unprecedented and humiliating step of publicly announcing at the Guildhall in London that there was no truth in the rumour that he was intending to marry his niece.

Richard's problems might have been eased if a plot to seize Richmond in Brittany had succeeded. But Richmond escaped to France in August 1484 where he found his plans for organising an invasion of England given full support. By the summer of 1485 active preparations for war were underway. Early in August, with 3,000 French troops, Richmond set sail. Landing at Milford Haven on 7 August, he took a roundabout route through Wales and, gathering support as he marched, finally on 22 August came face to face with the king near Market Bosworth in Leicestershire. The king himself might well have welcomed the opportunity to deal a final blow to the alliance of excluded Yorkists and die-hard Lancastrians who opposed him. A decisive victory could well have established him securely on the throne and enabled him to make a fresh start. What precisely decided the battle in Richmond's favour is not entirely clear. He was outnumbered on the field, but had the support of Lord Stanley and his brother William at the critical moment. Yet the king was anticipating this treachery. It is possible that Henry Percy, earl of Northumberland, who commanded one unit of the royal army, refused to engage; or alternatively the forces might have been so arrayed that it was impossible for him to join the fray. In the event an impetuous charge by Richard at his rival's standard in the hope of deciding the issue quickly gave the opportunity for his enemies to close in for the kill. When the battle was over Henry Tudor had emerged the improbable victor and the wearer of the crown.

As with his predecessors, it took Henry VII a long time to secure his throne. Although he presented himself as the unifier and healer of old wounds, there were many who refused to accept the change of regime. Ricardian sympathy was strong in the north. There was a rising in the spring of 1486, which quickly fizzled out, but several of those involved preferred to take to the Cumbrian fells before submitting in the autumn. A more serious challenge came in 1487 behind the name of the imposter Lambert Simnel who claimed to be Edward, earl of Warwick, the son of George, duke of Clarence, held by the king in the Tower. This rising which again received substantial support in north-east England, was crushed on the field of Stoke, near Newark in Nottinghamshire. More trouble occurred in 1489 in the north, when the earl of Northumberland was killed in a tax riot, partly it was said because he was blamed for betraying Richard III. Three years later another imposter emerged, Perkin Warbeck, who claimed to be the younger of the two princes who had disappeared in 1483. Supported by Margaret, duchess of Burgundy, and exploited by the Scots the would-be Richard IV remained on the scene, a thorn in Henry VII's side, for several years. Even after Warbeck's capture and death, along with the unfortunate earl of Warwick in 1499, Henry faced intrigue and plots in the name of the house of York which focused on the remaining descendants of Edward IV, members of the de la Pole family in exile. It is easy for historians to dismiss these imposters and intrigues as trivial, but Henry VII himself did not. He knew only too well how a twist of fortune could turn an apparently hopeless cause into a triumphal victory. Moreover the death of his queen and his first and third sons in quick succession in 1501–3, leaving only an eleven-year-old boy to carry the hopes of his dynasty, intensified his sense of insecurity. The king's propaganda had as much immediacy and pertinence towards the end of his reign as at the beginning.

Ultimately it was to become apparent, perhaps not until after the unchallenged succession of Henry VIII in 1509, that Henry VII had indeed succeeded in restoring dynastic stability and even monarchical authority. That indefinable quality of general credibility and natural acceptance as the unquestioned regime – achieved by Henry V after Agincourt and by Edward IV after Tewkesbury – came slowly to the Tudors. In retrospect, however, the battle of Stoke came to be seen as a decisive confirmation of the result of Bosworth. The Wars of the Roses had for all practical purposes come to an end then.

Summary: the character of the wars

The events we have recounted had three separate but overlapping characteristics: that of dynastic struggle; that of factional conflict between 'ins' and 'outs'; and that of a series of private vendettas. The term 'Wars of the Roses' is explicitly dynastic. Interpreted dynastically there were but two wars: Lancaster against York and York against Tudor. In an important sense the second was also a war within the house of York between Richard of Gloucester and his heirs, real and feigned, on the one hand and Edward IV's heirs, ultimately Elizabeth of York, on the other. As the champion of the rights of Elizabeth of York, Henry VII was an adopted Yorkist. The support he received from exhousehold men of Edward IV and Edward V was in practice far more important in his campaign to win and to hold the throne than his die-hard Lancastrian following. This characteristic of Henry VII's political position was well understood by the Crowland continuator who wrote in 1486 that 'the tusks of the boar had been blunted and the red rose, *the avenger of the white*, shines upon us' (my italics). For this well-placed writer it was not a question of the red rose overcoming the white: on the contrary the red took common cause with the white against the boar (Richard III). One cannot go to the extent of suggesting that these second wars were fought merely between York and York: Henry VII was nobody's tool. Thus they were wars between York and the new dynasty, Tudor, which profited from the internal dissension of its rival.

None of the Wars of the Roses was solely dynastic. Contained within them and in all cases leading up to them was the more commonplace strife between 'ins' and 'outs'; between a Court faction in power and a rival, excluded faction. The first wars arose out of such conflict between a Beaufort–Angevin Court faction and an excluded Yorkist faction. The attempts of Richard, duke of York, until March 1452 to profit from the debacle of

1449–50 by forcing himself upon a reluctant king as his natural adviser did not lead to civil war. The king held fast, Somerset succeeded to the position of trust held by Suffolk and York was excluded. Civil war only came after the king's mental breakdown and York's first protectorate. Having once tasted power in 1454 York was naturally unwilling to relinquish it. Thus the first battle of St Albans was a preliminary round of open fighting for dominance at Court which was renewed in 1459 when Queen Margaret took steps to remove York and his friends once and for all. The campaigning and fighting which occurred between September 1459 and July 1460 were concentrated on the issue of who would control the Court, the king and the government. The question of the throne itself arose as a last resort for York and his friends who had come to realise that they would never be secure or able perpetually to rule in the name of a captive Henry VI.

Precisely the same development occurred in 1469–70, although more rapidly. Warwick was the excluded magnate who went to war to enforce his services on Edward IV. Within six months he was plotting to depose Edward and place Clarence on the throne. Within eighteen months he had succeeded in restoring Henry VI. The events of 1483–87 similarly have the characteristic of 'ins' v. 'outs'. It cannot be argued that Richard of Gloucester was an excluded politician in the last month of Edward IV's reign. Any magnate who has a county palatine created for him, as Gloucester had in Cumberland in January 1483, must, on the contrary, be considered highly favoured. In Gloucester's mind in April 1483 there may have been fear of *future* exclusion, but he was not at the time excluded. On the other hand, Gloucester's constant companion and seconder in the revolution was an excluded politician. Henry, duke of Buckingham, had been pointedly left out of Edward IV's charmed circle. For him Richard III's usurpation was, if nothing else, the means to royal favour, high office and power. Moreover Richard III's acts dispossessed many; not only members of the Woodville family and associates of Lord Hastings, but also the greater part of Edward IV's household. For them Bosworth offered the opportunity of returning to office and influence.

41

There is no need to belabour the point that civil wars are extensions of factional politics. There was, however, a third element involved in the Wars of the Roses which gave them a particularly sharp edge: the matter of vendetta. Disputes over property and local domination were frequent in late-medieval society. It was one of the responsibilities of royal government to stifle and settle such disputes which erupted between the more powerful subjects so as to prevent lawlessness and disorder getting out of hand. The England of Henry VI was riven by many such disputes, as for instance between Moleyns and Paston in East Anglia, Harrington and Stanley in Lancashire or Talbot and Berkeley in Gloucestershire. In these, and many others, a disputed inheritance lay at the heart of the quarrel. In others, potentially more dangerous, local lords competed for local domination. Such was the conflict between Bonville and Courtenay in Devon and Percy and Neville in the north. In the 1450s several disputes were allowed to develop out of control. And, in a society in which the code of honour was still strong, once rivalry had led to the taking of arms and the taking of arms to the shedding of blood, dispute ran into feud. Pursued during the wars, and ultimately subsumed in them, was a series of personal vendettas. The prosecution of these feuds introduced an element of animosity and ruthlessness which from time to time superceded all else.

The dominant feud was that between the houses of Beaufort and York, both branches of the royal house. York's resentment against, and bitter condemnation of, Edmund Beaufort, duke of Somerset in 1450 stemmed not so much from thwarted ambition, let alone concern for the common good, but from personal animosity generated in their rivalry for command in France. From 1450 onwards Beaufort and York pursued each other with a venom which reached its denouement at St Albans, when Somerset was hacked down by men serving in York's cause. Thereafter Somerset's heir, Henry, the new duke, was bent on a revenge achieved at Wakefield on the last day of 1460, disposing not only of York, but also his second son, the sixteen-year-old Edmund, earl of Rutland. Somerset himself escaped the carnage of Towton three months later and continued the fight against

Edward IV from Northumberland until the end of 1462. But then, in a dramatic and much publicised act of reconciliation in 1463, Somerset was pardoned, restored and taken into high favour by the king. Nevertheless, despite all Edward IV's efforts, Somerset deserted him again at the first opportunity in December of the same year. Taken at Hexham in April 1465 he was immediately executed. Edward IV's generosity to Somerset has tended to puzzle historians. It need not. It was both an act of policy and an act of personal magnanimity by the king intended to end the blood feud between the two families. Edward thereby forwent his right of revenge for the deaths of his father and brother. Blood brotherhood, as symbolised by the duke being given the honour of sharing the king's bed chamber, was to replace blood feud. The king's subsequent bitter condemnation of Somerset's new betrayal as being 'against nature of gentleness and all humanity' reveals that honour as much as policy was at stake. Somerset himself may have been motivated in part by undying loyalty to Henry VI, but he probably also found that he could not that easily forgive and forget the wrongs done to his family by the house of York.[8] He paid the price. And so did his brother and heir Edmund at Tewkesbury in 1471. For twenty years Beaufort and York pursued each other until the male line of Beaufort was obliterated.

The blood feud between Beaufort and York was not the only one to divide the political nation in mid-fifteenth-century England. Neville and Percy too were at each other's throats. The Neville–Percy feud arose out of competition for dominance in the north, but became more bitter and personal because of a dispute over the future of the manor of Wressle in the East Riding. In 1453 a private war broke out between the two families. This private war continued on the field of St Albans in 1455, which was as much a part of the Neville–Percy conflict as a confrontation between York and Beaufort. At St Albans Henry Percy, earl of Northumberland was killed: five years later his younger son, Thomas, Lord Egremont fell at Northampton. Egremont's brother, the third earl inherited an obligation to seek the revenge of two deaths. This was achieved after Wakefield when Salisbury was taken and executed and his younger son

Thomas killed in the battle. Three months later Northumberland himself and a younger son Richard were cut down by the avenging Neville brothers, Warwick and Montagu, at Towton. In 1464 yet another son of the dead earl was killed at Hedgeley Moor. A third blood feud was settled in 1460–61; that between Lord Bonville and the earl of Devon. Such feuds even extended into families, for Neville was divided against Neville. Ralph Neville, earl of Westmorland, had partitioned his inheritance between families by his two countesses, the junior branch, whose mother was a Beaufort, taking the lion's share. The senior branch, the earls of Westmorland, were understandably reluctant to accept this disinheritance which virtually left them with estates only in the county palatine of Durham. In 1459 they took the side of Beaufort and Percy against York and their half brothers. The second earl of Westmorland himself was incapacitated, the initiative falling on the shoulders of his brothers, Sir John, who fought at Wakefield and had a hand in the death of the earl of Salisbury, and Thomas of Brancepeth. Sir John in his turn fell at Towton. The mantle ultimately fell on the shoulders of Thomas's son Sir Humphrey Neville of Brancepeth, the earl's nephew, who maintained a running battle, virtually single handed, against Warwick and Edward IV until he was taken and executed in 1469.

The Wars of the Roses therefore involved three overlapping elements: the vendetta, the factional and the dynastic from which they take their name. At periods of most intensive conflict, especially 1460–61, all three were entwined. The battles of these years were occasions in which personal scores were settled, in which the control of government was decided and ultimately at Towton the question of the ruling dynasty was determined. The element of personal vendetta was a developing characteristic: a consequence of rivalry and conflict after blood was shed. It helped extend and intensify the level of violence; but it was not an originating cause. The causes lay more deeply in the society and politics of fifteenth-century England.

3

THE CAUSES OF THE WARS

There were several interlocking reasons for outbreak of civil war in 1459. The precise weight to be given to each and balance to be struck between them has been, and will remain, a matter of controversy. Dynastic causes, the original idea that England fell into civil strife 'by reason of titles', has tended to receive short shrift at the hands of modern historians, but should not be dismissed out of hand. Arguments that the wars were caused either by economic and financial crisis in the ranks of the nobility, or by defeat in the Hundred Years' War have also tended to be unfashionable in recent years. Recent debate has largely focused on whether the wars resulted from a long-term shift in the balance of political power between Crown and greater subject, with a resultant increase in disorder and lawlessness, or whether they were largely the consequence of the shortcomings of Henry VI as king. These various factors can be perceived as long-term causes, rooted deeply in the development and structure of English society in the late middle ages; short-term causes, arising from more recent experience; and the immediate causes which actually led to civil war. The long-term developments may have made the wars possible, the short-term likely, but only the immediate certain. In the long-term the impact of 'bastard feudalism' and changes in the balance of power between Crown and subject are significant; in the short term, economic and financial pressures on English landholders, the consequences of defeat in the Hundred Years' War and the question of dynastic legitimacy are most relevant; and for the immediate the clash of personalities and the characters of Henry VI and his queen are central. These considerations apply specifically to the causes of the first wars. Most discussions of the causes of the Wars of the Roses tend to assume that what caused them can by extension be taken to have caused the second. This was not necessarily the case. The second wars, which broke out twelve years after the first ended, may have had different causes. With this in mind, the causes of the second wars will be considered separately at the end of this chapter.

Long-term causes of the first wars

The argument that bastard feudalism was the fundamental cause of the Wars of the Roses is second only to dynastic legitimacy in antiquity. Its development is particularly associated with Charles Plummer and William Denton in the late-nineteenth century. In the mid-fifteenth century, the argument ran, the government of England was paralysed by the overgrown power and insubordination of the nobles, especially overmighty subjects who were able to pursue their own private quarrels without let or hindrance. The origin of this evil was supposed to lie in the development of bastard feudalism in the reign of Edward III. After 1399 the government was 'controlled, if not directed', by half a dozen of these mighty peers. The wars resulted from the collapse of central control and were in effect a repetition on a large scale of those private wars which distracted almost every country.[1] The Victorian view was forcibly restated by Professor Storey in 1965. 'The civil wars were the outcome of this collapse of law and order' linked with the development of bastard feudalism 'a retrograde step', which 'threatened to destroy the constitutional and legal progress achieved since the twelfth century'. From the mid-fourteenth century 'the parasitic hold of "bastard feudalism" on royal justice grew stronger'. Lords, especially overmighty subjects, took the law into their own hands on behalf of their retainers. Under Henry VI '"bastard feudalism" developed without restraint'. All the conflicts both locally and at Court ultimately coalesced into one conflagration: 'the Wars of the Roses were thus the outcome of an escalation of private feuds'.[2]

An explanation of the outbreak of civil war in 1459 and the collapse of the Lancastrian regime which lays emphasis on a deep-rooted malaise in society contains two elements: the first the long-term shift in prestige, authority and power between king and greater subjects dating from the reign of Edward III; and the second the central and malign role of bastard feudalism in this deterioration. It would be as well to consider the two separately.

It has generally been accepted that under Edward I (d. 1307) the English monarchy reached the zenith of its medieval power: under him the centralising tendencies of a century and a half reached a peak. By enforcing royal justice on all subjects and by establishing an effective central administrative machine, the kings of England had achieved a degree of authority within their realm found in few other kingdoms. In England there were no great appanages such as the duchies of Brittany, Burgundy or even Acquitaine in which the rulers were themselves petty princes able to defy the king. Whereas France in the fourteenth century had to some extent the characteristic of a confederacy of princes under one head, England was unified. The Principality of Wales as the appanage of the heir to the throne was in effect annexed to the Crown. The county palatine of Durham under a bishop's rule was thereby amenable to royal control. While it would be wrong not to acknowledge the existence of many local liberties and privileges, it is nevertheless the case that for a medieval kingdom England by the fourteenth century was remarkably centralised. Her manageable size helped, but it was also the result of conscious policy.

The centralising drive of English kings had been resisted by their subjects. In the early-fourteenth century it became established that kings could not amend law without the consent of subjects represented in the new institution of parliament. Thus there developed a significant legal brake on the regality or absolute power of the sovereign. Financially, too, the Crown was relatively poorly endowed. During the fourteenth century it became established practice that the consent of parliament was necessary before taxes could be raised. The Crown did not command the resources in land to free itself from these restraints. Moreover the king, partly as a consequence of his lack of endowments, had no ultimate coercive power: he did not hold a monopoly of military force. Indeed he depended on his greater subjects to provide arms and armies when needed for defence of the realm. In the last resort, therefore, kings depended on consent. It was both necessary and desirable for a king to rule with and through his greater subjects who effectively controlled the localities. Thus, while administratively England was relatively centralised, politically harmony and civil order depended on the maintenance of a delicate balance between king and greater subject.

The strenuous and for a time successful efforts of Edward I to enhance his control over his kingdom ultimately led to conflict, intensified and worsened under his son Edward II. The first 40 years of the fourteenth century were characterised by this strife between Crown and baronage. After 1340 Edward III effected a remarkable transformation. This was achieved on the one hand by leading his disaffected and quarrelsome barons into victorious war against France, consciously developing a cult of chivalry with himself at its head. On the other hand Edward also secured their enthusiastic support for his war and happy collaboration by making a series of significant concessions to his barons. These included modification of the treason laws to reduce the levying of private war to mere felony; relaxation of the enforcement of central royal justice on the provinces and the development in its place of delegated administration of justice through Commissions of the Peace which were from the start dominated by the local landed élites; and allowing tenants-in-chief to gain more absolute control of their lands through the development of entailment and enfeoffments to use – in effect a partial abandonment of feudal rights. The status and prestige of the king's greater subjects was also enhanced by the development of the hereditary peerage defined by membership of the House of Lords, the creation of new titles such as duke and the marriage of his own children into the ranks of the upper peerage. Finally, so as to raise effective armies, he encouraged his greater subjects and companions in arms to recruit their own permanent military retinues.[3]

Edward III created an upper nobility, many of whose members became part of the royal family, all of whom were companions in arms, to whom he was less an overlord, more a first among equals. In his own heyday he was brilliantly successful, but later his policy proved damaging to the Crown. The cumulative effect was to surrender elements of judicial, financial, territorial and military power to magnates, some of whom were also of the blood royal and therefore enjoyed a further enhanced status. These men were mighty, potentially overmighty, subjects.

But it was by no means inevitable that Edward III's retraction of his father's and grandfather's heavy lordship should have led to the Wars of the Roses. An enhanced upper nobility and a wider royal family were potentially sources of strength to a king. Moreover it was open to Edward's successors to attempt to claw back some of his concessions. It is arguable that this is what Richard II unsuccessfully attempted to do and what, for a brief period, Henry V achieved. Richard II seems to have foundered because he was unable to win the trust of his magnates: Henry V to have triumphed because he inspired them. Ultimately in late-medieval politics the power and authority of the Crown depended on the character of the king and his personal relationships with his greater subjects. The political world was small, familial and claustrophobic. The institutions of the constitution, administration and the law were in the last resort only as strong as the personality of the monarch. A hereditary monarchy placed a special burden on the personal qualities of the man born to be king. An unstable and unpredictable man like Richard II, or a weak and feckless man like Henry VI, was always likely to place an intolerable strain on the political process. As K. B. McFarlane famously observed 'only an undermighty ruler had anything to fear from overmighty subjects'.[4]

Nevertheless, there is an important sense in which kings after Edward III were institutionally less mighty than kings before him. For he had allowed the gap in power and prestige to narrow. If not impossible, he made it more difficult for his successors to enforce their authority. He put greater stress on the personal qualities and capacity of the king. This is revealed in the experience of Richard II who, in his attempt to recover lost authority, resorted to asserting his prerogative and regality above his subjects while at the same time building up his own household and retinue (under the famous badge of the white hart) in competition with his greater subjects. Although he claimed in theory to be above his subjects, in practice he behaved as if he were one. No doubt Richard's own strange personality led him down this fatal path, but it is arguable that his grandfather's heritage pointed in that direction. Henry IV, by virtue of his usurpation, was in no position, even if he had the inclination, to attempt to recover lost ground. Henry V proved that an exceptional man could still rule effectively but his achievement proved to be a fleeting phenomenon. The long minority of his son was clearly not conducive to a revival of independent royal authority. Fate and circumstances thus conspired to perpetuate what Edward III had conceded.

Thus it is arguable that by the mid-fifteenth century, as a result of Edward III's policy, the balance of power between Crown and mighty subject had shifted marginally yet critically in favour of the subject. What role did bastard feudalism play in this? The argument is that, by allowing the formation of armed followings, the development of the indentured retinue created the means by which mighty subjects could take the law into their own hands and subvert the Crown. There is no doubt that, as a means of supplying troops to fight his wars, the practice of recruiting followers by indentured retainers became widespread during the reign of Edward III. It was continued under Henry V and Henry VI. But bastard feudalism and indentured retainers have to be put in perspective. The very phrase, as invented by Charles Plummer, with its sense of illegitimacy and debasement implied that earlier feudalism had been legitimate and honourable. There is however no a priori reason for holding that relationships between lord and vassal in earlier times were any more stable, or that the feudal lords were any less threatening to monarchs than bastard feudal lords. Indeed in one respect bastard feudalism might be thought to be more sophisticated. The substitution of a money fee for land as the means for binding man to lord gave the lord greater flexibility and ease of control. It was easier to stop a fee than to reoccupy a manor. Secondly, as is argued in the next chapter, the practice of retaining by indenture did not create large private armies. Indeed K. B. McFarlane was at pains, especially in his later work, to point out that retaining was as much for peace as for war: lawyers and estate administrators were retained as frequently as soldiers; and local gentry were expected to give counsel, attend household festivals and to support their lords at great occasions of state as much as they were to don armour and to do battle. Thirdly there has been a tendency to exaggerate the significance of indentured retaining. The formal contract of service was but one element involved in the construction of an affinity surrounding a great lord. There were many others attached to and attracted to a lord in addition to those formally retained or granted annuities. These 'well-willers', like more formally retained knights and esquires, were anxious to secure his patronage by doing good service in return for good lordship.

The affinity of a great lord (his household, indentured retinue and well-willers) was the organisation through which the social, administrative and political life of his country operated as well as being the means by which the lord himself sought to impress upon the king his own indispensability.[5] Much of the lawlessness associated with retaining in fact resulted not from the practice itself but from the illegal temporary raising of gangs and the distribution of badges and liveries to men hired by the day to assault an enemy or attack his property. Such was the case at Bakewell, Derbyshire on 23 February 1468 when John Talbot, third earl of Shrewsbury distributed his badge – a white dog – to nineteen or more local lads, recruited to attack Lord Grey of nearby Codnor.[6] This abuse was the target of the series of laws against retaining passed from 1390. Contemporaries well understood the dangers involved in unlimited and casual retaining: the law sought to restrict it to a privilege enjoyed by peers, allowing, other than household servants or lawyers, only the retaining of knights and esquires for life. The laws may not always have been effectively enforced, but laxity was a result of the inability or unwillingness of the Crown to prosecute and not directly the consequence of retaining itself.

An affinity in fifteenth-century England worked in much the same way as a connection in eighteenth-century England. In other words, it was the particular form of a general system of patronage and clientage that was intrinsic to a patriarchal society. For this reason it could also act as a force for stability. It was in the interest of lords to keep their own followings in order and to deal with conflicts that arose between their retainers. Thus in 1465 John Paston and Sir Gilbert Debenham, in dispute over possession of a manor, threatened force against each other. The duke of Norfolk promptly stepped in because, as John Paston III observed, if allowed to go unchecked the matter would have been of great disworship to him 'considering how he taketh us both for his men and so we be known well enough'. The two were called to Framlingham and the duke patched up a settlement.[7] Similar examples of the fourth earl of Northumberland setting his own retinue in order are revealed in the Plumpton correspondence. Indeed it was not only retainers and well-willers who submitted themselves to the arbitration of lords. The expense of litigation being as it was, in all districts of England men were accustomed to having their differences resolved by the good offices of their local magnate.[8] In this respect, as it has often been observed, bastard feudalism could act as an influence for order and stability.[9]

It is nevertheless true that on some occasions and in some parts of England bastard feudalism could intensify instability and disorder. This might occur, as happened in Devon and Warwickshire in the 1440s and 1450s, when a once great affinity (those of the Courtenays and the Beauchamps) disintegrated and successor lords competed to take their place.[10] Or it might happen, as it did in Yorkshire in the 1450s, when two powerful magnates competed for domination of a district.[11] The most quoted example of the multiple fee-taking which has been taken to be the hallmark of inherent instability, that of Sir Humphrey Stafford of Grafton (fees worth £71 a year from eight different lords), comes from the former in Warwickshire. Another example cited by K. B. McFarlane, that of Sir James Strangways of West

Harlsey in Yorkshire, does not stand up to close analysis; for although Strangways did indeed take many fees and allow himself 'a commodious escape route', the fees were not paid by competing lords and when it came to a choice, he remained steadfastly loyal to his Neville lords.[12] In fact the retainers of both Neville and Percy, despite the upheavals in their fortunes, revealed themselves to be remarkably steadfast and loyal over several generations.

Bastard feudalism was in essence neutral. It could be a force for stability or for instability; it could be a vehicle of disorder and corruption or for order and legality. It very much depended on the local circumstances, on the personality of the lord and above all the power and authority of the monarch. A commanding and inspiring monarch such as Henry V could coordinate and channel the energies of lords and their affinities into directions which were not self-destructive. A feeble and ineffective king like Henry VI stood by hopelessly as lords and their affinities turned on one another. But his failure, no more than his father's success, was not the consequence of bastard feudalism as such. It was the consequence of political timidity.

Bastard feudalism, the form in which late-medieval patronage and clientage operated, was not a particular cause of civil war in the mid-fifteenth century. More important than the development of bastard feudalism itself was the broader shift in the balance of power between Crown and magnate which occurred concurrently and which made it critically harder for the Crown to impose restraint on errant mighty subjects. Restraint was not impossible to achieve as the careers of both Henry V and later, Edward IV reveal; one may conclude, however, that it became more difficult and placed a heavier demand on the personal aptitude of the king. To this extent longer-term socio-political causes had a part to play in the Wars of the Roses.

Short-term causes of the first wars

Economic change taking place in England after 1350 may have

53

added to the difficulties facing the Crown. The question of economic causes of the Wars of the Roses has been almost as hotly disputed as the socio-political roots. Until the twentieth century the observable economic recession of the fifteenth century tended to be seen as a consequence not a cause of the general malaise affecting English society. It was the late Sir Michael Postan who in 1939 suggested that agricultural depression hit landlords hardest and surmised that dwindling revenues contributed to the 'political gangsterdom' of the age. It is clear from the passage that Postan had private feuding in mind. But in 1954 Ross and Pugh extended the analysis to suggest that financial crisis prompted lords to compete more desperately for the patronage of the Crown in the form of grants of land, offices and pensions. 'The Wars of the Roses were fought, it would seem, not because magnates could afford to hire armies of retainers to fight their battles, but rather because they could no longer afford to pay them.'[13] In response McFarlane argued that although there may have been a general contraction in baronial wealth, because certain prominent lords enjoyed the revenues of several combined inheritances, they were considerably wealthier than their fathers. Falling rents did not necessarily mean a poorer family: more manors compensated for lower yields. Thus he concluded that for the leading participants financial difficulty was not a consideration.[14]

McFarlane was undoubtedly correct concerning the enhanced personal wealth of York, Richard Neville, earl of Warwick, and Humphrey Stafford, duke of Buckingham. But the conclusion is arguably not true of Henry Percy, earl of Northumberland, who had difficulty recovering all his estates after the forfeiture of 1408; and certainly not of Edmund Beaufort, duke of Somerset who enjoyed a pitifully small landed estate. Moreover three magnates – York, Warwick and Buckingham all held extensive estates in the Welsh marches. In Wales English landlords faced what was in effect a land war: a general refusal to pay feudal dues and fines which had once provided a lucrative source of revenue. This boycott was more political than economic in genesis, but it had a similarly damaging impact on finances.[15] Furthermore, even in respect of revenue from land, magnates such as York, Buckingham and Warwick were well aware that their predecessors had once enjoyed higher revenue from individual estates and were themselves experiencing, even in their own lifetime, a continuing fall in landed income. They may, as McFarlane stressed, have increased pressure on their administrators to produce more;[16] but this did not necessarily preclude the parallel pursuit of compensation from royal favour. In northern England in particular landed revenues were reduced by approximately ten per cent following the agrarian crisis of 1438–40 and it can be shown that some landlords were still suffering from the effects of this in the 1450s.[17] There is no reason to doubt that these adverse circumstances affected Richard Neville, earl of Salisbury and Henry Percy, earl of Northumberland, intensifying the rivalry between them which burst into the open in the early 1450s. Indeed the immediate cause of open fighting was a dispute over the possession of Wressle, part of the old Percy inheritance, which Salisbury was attempting to acquire for one of his younger sons.[18] In the 1450s royal favour was of critical material importance to all magnates.

Economic and financial difficulties also affected the Crown. During Richard II's reign regular royal revenue was approximately £120,000 per annum. By the last five years of Henry VI's reign it had fallen by possibly as much as two-thirds to approximately £40,000. These are very approximate numbers based on exchequer figures. The sum for the last years of Henry VI is particularly unreliable since by then much royal income was bypassing the exchequer. Although the actual total of revenue being received is impossible to calculate, it is nevertheless clear that in the 1450s royal finances were in chaos, the king's credit was negligible and the Crown was virtually bankrupt. There were several causes of this, and much of the responsibility can be laid at the king's door. But his own extravagance and profligacy was not the sole cause. During the first half of the century the Crown suffered a serious loss of revenue at source, both in the yield of crown lands (a problem shared with its greater subjects) and in the return from customs and subsidies. This latter was of critical importance for the Crown was the victim of a trade depression which it could not control.[19]

The collapse of royal finances under Henry VI had profound implications both for his ability to assert his authority over his subjects and for his capacity to satisfy their intensifying demands on him. But equally important, the underlying economic trend and its financial implications for the Crown would have made it more difficult for any king to cope whatever his personal abilities. By mid-fifteenth century the monarchy was not only politically weaker but also financially more stretched in comparison with its greater subjects than it had been 100 years earlier.

One of the causes of the bankruptcy of the Lancastrian dynasty in the 1450s was the burden of war. Lacking the necessary resources of its own, fighting an unsuccessful war which failed to pay for itself, being able to call only upon restricted and limited levels of taxation from its subjects, saddled with mounting debts and increasingly unable to raise new loans, the Crown was the principal financial loser in the later stages of the war in France. Defeat in Normandy in 1450 and Gascony in 1453, leaving only Calais in English hands, is another possible cause of the outbreak of civil war. After all, it is often observed that failure in foreign war is a cause of domestic disturbances. As with other aspects of this subject recent historical opinion has been divided. Some like McFarlane have played down the impact of defeat in war on domestic politics; others, notably Keen, have given it a decisive weight.[20]

The whole question of war and society in fifteenth-century England is highly germane. Developing the statement made by the chancellor in parliament in 1474 that 'justice, peace and prosperity hath continued anywhile in this land in any king's days but in such as hath made war outward', Dr Richmond has argued that it was the very ending of war in France itself (whether in defeat or victory is immaterial) which opened the flood gates of civil war.[21] The chancellor's statement of 1474 was to an extent demonstrably true. England was without doubt internally more peaceful between 1415 and 1450 because many unruly elements, high as well as low born, were able to exercise their martial talents at the expense of the French. But a wider issue is also raised. War not peace, it is argued, was the natural pursuit of the fifteenth-century nobleman. A gentleman was educated to find virtue and nobility in the vocation of war not in the arts of peace. Chivalry, the idealisation of warfare as the highest goal in a layman's life, was a powerful cultural force.[22] It needed an outlet. Henry V's generation had had ample opportunity to demonstrate its prowess. The survivors of this generation, such as John Talbot, earl of Shrewsbury, Sir John Fastolf and Sir William Oldhall, were ageing veterans passing the way of all flesh in the 1450s. Certainly there was a vocal body of opinion, articulated by Fastolf's secretary William Worcester, who argued for a continuation of war against the French to rekindle the embers of dying chivalry and thereby restore social harmony.[23]

But for whom exactly did Worcester speak? For no-one, bar a small group of passé ultra-conservatives, is one answer. Even during the early years of Henry VI's reign his government had difficulty persuading gentlemen actually to serve in France. The interests of the great majority of English landed society were shifting from military to civilian pursuits. As Worcester himself recognised, his age was the age of the gentleman bureaucrat seeking advancement not through profession of arms but the professions of law and accountancy. The entertainment, literature and outward display of the later-fifteenth-century gentleman may still have been ostensibly chivalric in form and style, but his actual life interests were increasingly civilian.[24]

There can be little doubt that there were men of both kinds in the 1450s. For lack of conclusive evidence we cannot tell which formed the majority. There may have been a regional difference. In England north of the Trent, where the Scottish menace was perceived as ever present, the values of chivalry may have been more tenaciously maintained than in more southerly counties. But men trained in the school of chivalry, from north or south, were more likely to settle their differences by violent means. To this extent at least the absence of outward war may have helped create the climate in which a resort to arms to settle political differences was more likely.

More specifically, it is clear that defeat in France itself did not lead immediately to the outbreak of the Wars of the Roses. By far the most traumatic shock for the realm as a whole, if not for Henry VI himself, was suffered after the loss of Normandy in 1450. This was not only because Normandy was nearer, because many Englishmen had vested interests in its continuing possession, or because in English hands it had been a shield protecting the Channel and securing the seas; it was also because Normandy was the conquest of Henry V and its loss most directly pointed out the contrast between father and son. In 1450 the defeat led to the most serious crisis, both parliamentary and extra-parliamentary, that had shaken the Crown since 1381. It brought down Suffolk's government and led to popular revolt. The whole regime was severely threatened. But it recovered. By 1452 Henry VI's reign seemed to be on a surer footing than before. The loss of Gascony in 1453 caused no equivalent upheaval. By 1455, it would seem, the realm as a whole had accepted defeat.

Yet if defeat in France was not a direct cause of the outbreak of sustained civil war in 1459, it is possible that it had an indirect material and political impact which later contributed to the wars. It can no longer be argued that the loss of Normandy brought home 'thousands of household retainers, with nothing to do but brawl and bully'.[25] Most of these veterans were discharged and, being penniless and homeless, their plight tended to excite the pity rather than the fear of contemporaries.[26] The circumstances of their captains is harder to assess, for it is not at all clear whether these men returned from the wars impoverished or enriched. McFarlane argued consistently that the captains, unless they were exceptionally unlucky, were able to continue to profit from the wars until the bitter end.[27] But while it is true that some prominent commanders were able to ship home their profit for investment in England well before the tide turned and others were still taking substantial profit from land, office and loot in the 1440s, the numerous cases of the less fortunate should not be overlooked. Sir Thomas Dring, for example, who first served under Henry V, was captured and ransomed no fewer than six times, the last occasion being at Formigny in 1450. Dring might have joined Sir Robert James as one of the 26 alms knights of St George's, Windsor (the last resting place of distressed chivalry), who had been taken 4 times and then lost all his goods when Bayeux fell in 1450. At a more prominent level the veteran peers, who were field commanders, Lord Fauconberg and Lord Scales were both captured and ransomed in 1449–50. Scales had previously lost all his treasure when his fortress of Granville fell to the French in 1442.[28]

For those still serving in the field in 1449–50 the defeat was an unmitigated disaster. But even for those who might have escaped with their fortunes intact, by McFarlane's logic, the loss of what had proved to be a lucrative source of profit is likely to have been resented. In other words, whether the wars in France had proved in particular cases to have been profitable or ruinous the government's failure to hold Normandy was potentially a source of grievance.

Furthermore certain magnates came out of the war owed substantial sums of money by the Crown for their wages. The dukes of Buckingham and York and earl of Shrewsbury all presented large bills to the Crown, and, as creditors have throughout the ages, accepted partial settlement from their bankrupted debtor. It was not just arrears of wages for France that were outstanding. The earls of Salisbury and Northumberland and Lord Fauconberg had continual difficulty seeking payment for their Scottish border garrisons.[29] These royal debts intensified the need for these magnates, on behalf of themselves, their friends and their dependents, to be close to the king so as to receive preferential treatment at the exchequer and to maintain at least a chance of securing payment of even the negotiated reduced sums. Thus military debts added another reason to depressed land revenues for certain magnates to be more anxious for access to the Court. It is not to be thought that these magnates themselves were facing bankruptcy: their capital reserves were untouched. Yet the finances of several were in a state of some confusion and many faced a 'cash-flow' crisis. Crown debts underwrote their own credit. Favour was thus of crucial significance in keeping them afloat.

In a more directly political way the loss of Normandy had a bearing on the events of the 1450s. It was over Normandy that the two royal dukes, Richard of York and Edmund Beaufort, duke of Somerset fell out. The rift occurred partly because

Somerset was preferred for the post of lieutenant-governor in 1447 and partly because York lost substantial French possessions as a result of Somerset's negligence. From York's point of view it was not just a question of pique that he had been overlooked in 1447. He had a personal appanage in Normandy and as the previous governor an established affinity based in the province. The loss of his appanage, while he was himself prevented by his sojourn in Ireland from defending it in person, and without Somerset lifting a finger on his behalf, added insult to injury. When York returned to England in the summer of 1450 he was a man with a score to settle.[30]

York was not without support. There were others who had lost out to Somerset and his friends. In the last years of Lancastrian Normandy the duchy, like England itself, had divided into factions. One group, prominent among whom were the earl of Shrewsbury, Lord Hoo and Lord Scales had entered Somerset's circle and found no difficulty in sustaining their favour at Court after 1450. Others, of whom Sir William Oldhall, Sir Edmund Mulso and Sir William Retford might be cited remained York's men, and shared exclusion with him after 1450.[31] Rivalry and conflict set up in Normandy in the last few years of Lancastrian rule was brought back to England after its fall.

Somerset's responsibility for the loss of Normandy remained a potent source of propaganda for York and his friends which they steadfastly kept alive throughout the 1450s. York clothed himself in the robe of the lost leader who would have saved the French possessions had he been given the chance; as late as 1459 and 1460 he was still harking back to the negligence of the Court earlier in the decade. How much impact this propaganda had is another matter. Dr Keen has suggested that the humiliation suffered by Henry VI and the dent to national pride was an important reason for the collapse of the credibility of the Lancastrian regime.[32] It is to be suspected, however, that after 1455 the shame and dishonour was felt only by that part of the political nation still committed to the chivalric ethic and that, as propaganda, York's case only had a wider appeal to the people of Kent and neighbouring south-eastern counties now vulnerable, as they discovered, to renewed French raids. Even if it was no more than this (for in the last resort it is not possible to gauge how deeply into the soul of the realm humiliation in France cut) the loss of Normandy and Gascony was clearly yet another factor contributing to the collapse of Lancastrian prestige.

As the credibility of Henry VI's government came under attack from so many quarters and his capacity to satisfy the demands of his subjects became increasingly doubted, so the question of his right to the throne came to be raised. Most recent scholars have tended to dismiss the question of legitimacy as irrelevant to the actual causes of civil war. The idea that the dynastic issue was a side issue, at least until openly proclaimed by York in 1460, has tended to find wide support. However, as Professor Griffiths has shown, Henry VI and his advisers proved to be remarkably sensitive about his dynastic position while he had no heir apparent to the throne.[33] It is arguable too that the hostility shown to York between 1447 and 1453, when he was heir presumptive, was given an extra edge by the knowledge that he could, as heir to Mortimer as well as Edmund of Langley, mount a plausible alternative claim. This might account for the harsh treatment meted out to York's councillor, Thomas Young, when he proposed in parliament in May 1451 that York should be formally recognised as heir. If York himself at this time had no apparent intentions on the throne, it seems that Henry and his closest advisers did not entirely discount that possibility. What went on in York's mind we cannot tell. Mr Pugh has recently asserted that he 'had long regarded himself as rightful king of England'. York did, however, have a long-standing family grievance against the house of Lancaster. His father had been shabbily treated by Henry IV and Henry V, had plotted to overthrow Henry V in 1415 in favour of a Mortimer candidate and had paid the price. York was four when his father was executed. After the death of his uncle Edward, duke of York at Agincourt and of his uncle Edmund Mortimer, earl of March ten years later, he inherited both vast estates and the residual claim of the Mortimers in whose name plots had been laid until 1415.[34] To anyone with a keen sense of dynasty, as Henry VI

61

apparently had, York was likely to appear to be a potential threat. After the birth of Edward, Prince of Wales in 1453, Queen Margaret began to play a more assertive role in politics. By the end of the decade, and before York advanced his claim, it became apparent that her actions were determined as much by a desire to preserve her son's inheritance as by a need to prop up her husband's crumbling regime. York may have harboured hopes of advancement before November 1460: politically as important were the royal fears and suspicions, whether well grounded or not, that he aimed that far. In the event such fears became a self-fulfilling prophecy.

Immediate causes of the first wars

Discussion of the immediate causes of the Wars of the Roses focuses on the personality and mental health of Henry VI. As all historians agree, in the medieval political world the individual character of the king was paramount. Ultimately all hung on what kind of a man a monarch was. Henry VI was perhaps the most unfitted to rule of all the kings of England since the Norman conquest.[35] Henry was weak, vacillating, feckless and profligate. At all times he seems to have been like putty in the hands of those nearest to him: a man who always agreed with the last to have spoken with him, he created confusion by contradictory policy decisions and duplicated grants. He seems to have been fundamentally uninterested in the business of ruling and decision making; happy to grant away lands and annuities to all who importuned him, he was equally generous with pardons to those who offended him or broke his laws. After he came of age in 1437 he quickly fell into the hands of a faction, led ultimately by the duke of Suffolk, who monopolised the court and dominated its proceedings. After Suffolk fell a reconstituted faction under the leadership of Edmund Beaufort, duke of Somerset took over.

To what extent Henry asserted his own ideas and policies it is extremely hard to tell. He clearly abhorred warfare: a quality not likely to be appreciated in chivalric circles of a society embroiled in war at the time. His own preference was for peace with France, and the efforts made to find a formula for lasting peace after 1439 probably owe much to his desire for that end. But he never displayed the capacity or tenacity necessary to work effectively to achieve such a goal. He vaguely desired the end, but was incapable of developing the means. His initiative and personal impact have been discerned in the disastrous decision in 1446 to surrender Maine without a quid pro quo, perhaps to please his new queen. From time to time in the early 1450s he asserted himself, but to little lasting effect, in attempts to restore social harmony at home. Perhaps it would have been better for his kingdom had Henry been a complete pawn in the hands of his advisers, but his own independent interventions seem to have made matters difficult even for those on whom he relied. It has been suggested that Henry possessed a mean and vindictive streak, revealed particularly in his treatment of Humphrey, duke of Gloucester in 1447.[36] However, in a political world where all is done in the king's name regardless of whether he himself had knowledge of it, responsibility for decisions is hard to place. The vindictiveness is as likely to have been that of his favourites as his.

One thing is certain however, until 1453 Henry was not a simpleton or mentally ill. He was simply incompetent. Perhaps the key to Henry's personality lies, as has been argued, in his distinctive combination of piety and learning. Our picture of Henry as a person is coloured by the account given by his chaplain John Blacman who deliberately painted a picture of a man of Christian virtues, especially the virtues associated with the lay piety of the fifteenth century. Significant details in his biographical reminiscences can be independently validated and suggest that Henry was indeed more concerned with the next world than this; that he did prefer to dress and live simply; and that he was not only chaste but also extremely prudish. In Blacman's account Henry is presented as a paradigm of contemporary lay piety. This is distorting but not untruthful. Thus his public vices – his indiscriminate largesse, his reluctance to enforce the law and his erratic attitude to public affairs – are presented as private virtues. Indeed, it is possible that the purpose of the *Collectarium* (Blacman's biography) is to show that a higher virtue lay in being a bad king: he became a 'fool of

God'. Such a holy folly explains both the aura of sanctity that surrounds him and the political disasters that accompanied him.[37]

Blacman's account is problematic because it draws no distinction between the Henry who was sane but incompetent before 1453, and the Henry who was periodically insane but always mentally incapacitated as well as increasingly withdrawn from active involvement in the affairs of his kingdom, after that date. 1453 was a decisive watershed in the king's life and reign. There was a world of difference between a king who was incompetent and a king who was a simpleton. Until 1453 there was no apparent threat to his throne. After 1453, although long in gestation, this was ever more likely. It is only after 1453 that private feuding and wars in the provinces grew to alarming proportions; it is only after 1453 that faction at Court ran out of control; and it is only after 1453 that the government of the kingdom was reduced to being no more than the government of the victorious faction and its supporters.

War actually broke out in 1459 because Queen Margaret was by then finally in a position to attempt to destroy York and his friends once and for all. The emergence of Queen Margaret, a strong-willed young woman prepared to go to any extreme to protect the inheritance of her only son, marked the ultimate stage in the polarisation of factional conflict.[38] The queen, in a unique position to control king and Court, took over the leadership of the Beaufort faction after 1455. She was fully in command of the realm by the autumn of 1458. Thence both sides were openly preparing for the decisive confrontation. In the event over twelve years were to elapse before Lancaster was finally replaced by a securely established York.

At the heart of the debate about the causes of the first Wars of the Roses is the question of what precise weight to put on Henry VI's incapacity. All agree that it was significant. But for McFarlane his 'inanity' was all: if a king were undermighty, he wrote, 'his personal lack of fitness was the cause, not the weakness of his office and his resources'.[39] For Storey the weakness of the office was the fundamental cause. In terms of Henry VI's incapacity it is important to draw a distinction between his general inadequacy as a king before 1453 and his collapsed mental health after 1453. While Henry was mentally well but incompetent, factional strife developed but dynastic civil war was far off. The wars occurred in the circumstances created by Henry's mental incapacity. The English political system could not cope with a king who was neither totally insane nor really in good mental health. This, not the particular character of his personality before 1453, is the key to Henry VI's lack of personal fitness to rule. Besides this, the office was weaker in mid-fifteenth-century England and the resources available to the Crown were diminished. Any king, enjoying good health or not, successfully and effectively to rule his kingdom would have been more dependent on his own personal qualities than a king 100 years earlier. This is not to say that it would have been impossible to have been a successful monarch in the 1450s: the point is that it was more difficult and greater ability was demanded. To this extent the office was undermighty.

Whether we emphasise the office or the person, it was undoubtedly lack of royal authority, lack of government, lack of firm control from the centre which allowed private feuds and wars to grow unchecked and the kingdom to collapse into civil war. The paralysis at the centre enabled feuding to grow without restraint rather than the feuding inflict the paralysis on the centre. The Crown was unable to impose order. This is revealed most clearly by reference forward to the events of 1469–70 when Edward IV was temporarily unable to enforce his authority on the kingdom. At exactly those times when incapacitated by the opposition of Warwick and Clarence private feuds flared up again and subjects took the law into their own hands. In September 1469 the duke of Norfolk laid siege to Sir John Paston in Caister castle; in March 1470 a pitched battle took place at Nibley Green in Gloucestershire between Lord Berkeley and Lord Lisle; and later in the year during the Readeption Lord Stanley laid siege to the Harringtons in Hornby castle in Lancashire.[40] In 1469–70 private wars broke out after the collapse of royal government: they did not precede and create it.

In the mid-fifteenth century many circumstances combined to undermine the authority of the Crown – growing economic and financial pressures, material loss and humiliation in France, the lurking doubt concerning Henry VI's title. They made civil war more likely. In the last resort it was Henry's incapacity after 1453 which tipped the balance. In the end, to use a metaphor much favoured at the time, the ship of state was without a captain and, while the crew fell at each other's throats, she drifted onto the rocks.

The causes of the second wars

At the beginning of 1483 Englishmen and women could have been forgiven for thinking that the era of civil war and dynastic strife was over. Edward IV had apparently secured himself on the throne, he had two sons to provide for the future, and seemed to enjoy the support of a closely-knit, harmonious group of courtiers and councillors. Yet within six months, with a speed and from a quarter totally unexpected, this apparent stability was shattered. Even though its character was this time more of a broken sequence of murders, executions, armed insurrections and battles than of continuous, all-out war, once more England was plunged into an era of civil war. Whereas the wars of 1459–71 had arisen from a complex collapse of royal authority in which the mental incapacity of the king was a critical factor, the wars of 1483–87 followed a period of effective, authoritative kingship. Edward IV had without doubt begun the process of restoring the authority and strength of the Crown which had slipped in the years before his accession. As yet he had not been able, or had not had the inclination, to tackle some of the more fundamental structural weaknesses of monarchy inherited from Edward III. But he had taken steps to improve the financial position of the Crown and had benefited from a quickening of European trade and a rise in the income from customs. The Crown under Edward was financially stronger than under Henry VI. His landed subjects too were beginning to benefit from a recovery in rents and agricultural incomes. Edward had avoided major foreign entanglement and thus heavy taxation. More importantly by his general bearing, by his accustomed *bonhomie* and by his occasional ruthlessness (as in the destruction of his brother Clarence), he had stamped his personality on his kingdom. In his latter years he had nothing to fear from mighty subjects.

What, then, went wrong after Edward IV's early and sudden demise on 9 April 1483? Why did his son Edward V, aged twelve at the time, not survive to take over the rule of the kingdom some four or five years later? Although conventionally we are encouraged to consider that it is woeful for a land to be ruled by a child, in fact the precedents were hopeful. Richard II had inherited the kingdom at ten and had been unmolested. Henry VI was only nine months old on accession, but the political nation, if in disagreement over some matters, remained united on the point that nothing should prevent him entering his inheritance in both England and France. But Edward V was deposed within three months of his accession and before his coronation; and his deposition launched a new phase of civil war.

In recent years, especially following Dr Morgan's influential essay on the Yorkist polity, historians have emphasised the superficiality of Edward IV's achievement. His kingship even after 1471 relied too heavily on too small a group of trusted kinsmen and friends who were given substantial regional autonomy: Rivers in Wales and the marches; Gloucester in the far north and north-east; Stanley in Lancashire and Cheshire; Hastings in the north midlands; the marquis of Dorset in the south-west (after 1477).[41] This approach worked well while he was alive, held together as it was by the king's control over his Court. But beneath the surface, it is suggested, there were simmering jealousies and resentments which burst out the moment he was dead and which in their wake destroyed Edward V and plunged the kingdom once more into civil war.

It is no doubt true that Edward's regime contained within it the seeds of potential conflict. The magnates were able to consolidate their local power in the king's name, none more effectively so than his brother Richard of Gloucester in the north. Some benefits followed. In the north the old divisions between Percy and Neville, Neville and Neville were healed. The northern peerage and gentry became united behind the leadership of one very capable man. The quality of justice was improved and disorder quelled.[42] On the other hand, by 1483 Gloucester, like Rivers in Wales and the marches, had amassed a considerable strength which could be used as well against the Crown as for it. Moreover there were certain figures excluded and denied by the king, especially Henry Stafford, duke of Buckingham who found his ambitions in Wales and the Midlands thwarted by Rivers and Hastings.[43]

But it was not inevitable that these mighty subjects would turn on each other when Edward died. In fact the evidence for jealousies between them before the king's death is limited. There was little love lost between Dorset and Hastings because of rivalry over the captaincy of Calais (and possibly the favours of Mistress Shore). There is no evidence of conflict between Rivers and Gloucester: indeed they seem happily to have collaborated up to the king's death.[44] There may have been a coolness between Queen Elizabeth Woodville and Gloucester, but this is by no means certain. Moreover, even if the conflicts of April 1483, when Gloucester secured his role as Protector of the Realm, can be interpreted as the product of previously hidden tensions, it by no means follows that they should have led to the remarkable development of deposing the king. In no previous, or indeed later, minority where such rivalries also emerged did they so develop that the young king himself was deposed. What happened in 1483 was unique and not to be explained solely by the fact that Edward IV had allowed his principal supporters to become too powerful. Their power could have been employed, and the dead king had no doubt expected them to be employed, for the protection of his son and the preservation of his inheritance until the day he could enter it.

Edward IV's failure to renew the Hundred Years' War in 1475 has recently been put forward as the reason why his greater subjects turned on each other in 1483. Had there been outward war, there would have been no revival of inward war. Only a war in France could have finally removed the danger of a renewal of the Wars of the Roses by uniting all Englishmen in a common cause.[45] It is an attractive thesis. But it assumes that all Englishmen were indeed at one in desiring a revival of chivalric virtues; it assumes a second Agincourt and not a second Castillon; and it overlooks the contrasting diplomatic circumstances in 1415 and 1475. Only a successful resumption of war against France would have achieved the desired objective: unsuccessful war would have had the opposite effect. And Edward's judgement in 1475 that the time was not ripe was probably sound. Henry VII was later to show that it was possible to establish a secure regime without foreign entanglement. Moreover when Edward IV died there *was* a foreign war in progress. While it is true that the war launched by Edward IV against Scotland in 1480 did not develop into a war on the scale of the early-fourteenth century War of Independence, this was not for want of trying. Edward IV revived the English claim of sovereignty over Scotland, found a pliant alternative candidate for the throne, and launched a full-scale invasion. In 1482 Richard of Gloucester recovered Berwick, for those living north of the Trent no trivial achievement. In January 1483 Gloucester was said to be intending a major assault on south-west Scotland in the coming season. In other words, when Edward IV died England was engaged in outward war and the potential did exist for the political nation to find unity in facing a foreign foe. The reason why this was insufficient to prevent inward strife lay elsewhere.

A powerful lobby has long maintained that Edward V was reluctantly but rightly prevented from becoming king because of the shocking revelation of his illegitimacy. The renewal of civil war, by implication, thus resulted from the refusal of some to accept the truth. The truth or falsity of Richard III's claim that Edward V and his brother were bastards will never be known. The most recent and thorough examination of the case has revealed that it was thoroughly and skilfully put together, but tellingly concedes that 'the pre-contract story is plausible but not proved'.[46] This is the point. The accusation that Edward IV had been betrothed to Eleanor Butler before he married Elizabeth Woodville, thus making his children by her illegitimate, was not put to the verdict of a freely and properly convened ecclesiastical court. For this reason balanced judgement must remain, as most historians agree, that the claim was but a colour for an act of usurpation. Had Richard III been the deeply troubled, honourable and honest man we are asked to believe him to be he would surely either have followed the course of a properly constituted investigation, *or*, if the political circumstances precluded that, gone ahead with the coronation and made a subsequent parliamentary declaration of legitimacy. If parliament was competent to declare Edward V illegitimate, it was equally competent to declare him legitimate; as indeed a subsequent parliament declared Elizabeth I legitimate. The truth of the matter is that Richard III did not want Edward V to be legitimate because he did not want him to be king.

This leads us therefore to the only possible explanation of what happened in 1483: that Richard, duke of Gloucester, for whatever reason, determined to take the opportunity of his nephew's minority to seize the throne for himself. The second Wars of the Roses have but one ultimate explanation: they resulted from the action of one particular man. Considerable attention has been focused on Richard III's personality and the possible reasons for his behaviour in 1483; probably rightly so for what he did was both surprising and shocking. All surviving early accounts of his usurpation of the throne paint him as a hypocrite and a dissembler.[47] This contemporary and lasting image of duplicity is significant for it derives from the fact that no-one expected Richard of Gloucester, of all people, to raise his hand against his nephews. When his brother died he enjoyed an enviably high reputation as a man of honour and probity: a man to whom the protection of the young king could be fully entrusted. This, events soon showed, was a tragically mistaken appraisal of Richard. It explains both why he could take the throne so easily and also why, after the event, he was portrayed as having deliberately deceived the world while he plotted to achieve this end. Bearing in mind this understandable reaction of those who had been so wrong in their judgement of Richard of Gloucester, we need not now interpret his motives and action in the same manner.

But we will never fully understand why Richard III took such a step, fatal both to himself and to many of his contemporaries. It could have been naked ambition; an ambition perhaps only awakened after his brother's unexpected death. It could have been a calculated political step of attempted self-preservation. It is often surmised that he knew that he could not hope to retain the same influence at the Court of Edward V as he had at the Court of Edward IV and that he was 'getting his retaliation in first' – before he was excluded and before the king was crowned. Dr Hicks' careful examination of the title by which Richard held his estates, and ultimately upon which his power and influence stood, has shown that it was dangerously flawed and vulnerable to any loss of influence or revival in the fortunes of the male heirs of Warwick the Kingmaker. The future held many unknown risks. Indeed the timing of his decision to take the throne may have been determined by the largely unremarked upon death of George Neville, lately duke of Bedford, on 4 May 1483; a young man upon whose continued life Richard's hereditary title to his estates depended.[48] The usurpation may even have been ill-considered, hasty and impulsive. As has also been pointed out, there is much about Richard III's career which suggests that, far from being the Machiavellian schemer, he lacked any sound sense of political judgement. In which case, his usurpation stemmed not from unbridled lust for power but from a tragic lack of forethought.[49] Either way, Richard's action both destroyed himself and his dynasty. If he did take the throne for his own self-preservation, he failed lamentably in that objective.

Richard's actions created horror as well as surprise. During the course of the Wars of the Roses the perception of what was considered acceptable political behaviour had changed. Richard Neville, earl of Warwick was possibly responsible for introducing a more ruthless, less restrained attitude towards the lives of his enemies. He left a trail of executed or murdered rivals who had not been given the benefit of even a show trial. Edward IV had at least given his brother Clarence that. Richard of Gloucester's summary executions of Hastings, Rivers and Grey may not have been entirely unprecedented; although it has to be said that Warwick had dealt with his rivals after battle, not after lulling them into a false sense of security. But what quite clearly went beyond all bounds of conventional political morality in the late-fifteenth century was Gloucester's treatment of his nephews:

innocent children as it was frequently reiterated. Richard III
went one step further than was tolerated by even his own violent
age. The destruction of innocent children was beyond the limit
of acceptable political behaviour.[50] It does not matter that we
do not know the precise fate of the Princes in the Tower. It was
widely believed before the end of 1483 that they had met their
deaths; political realignment took place specifically on that
assumption. Richard III was held responsible by his contemporaries not just for the deposition of a rightful child king but also
for his and his brother's subsequent deaths. This condemnation
made it all the harder, although not impossible, for him to
succeed.

There is no call for virulent hostility to Richard III today any
more than there should be for excessive idolatory. Richard III's
career was more of a tragedy than a melodrama in which he
played the villainous uncle or virtuous hero. He was, there is no
reason to doubt, a man of great ability, highly respected for his
conventional virtues by his contemporaries.[51] Yet something
went wrong in 1483. Precisely what and why we will never
understand. What he did, for whatever reason, reopened the
wounds which his brother had apparently healed and destroyed
his own life and reputation. 'Had he suffered the children to
have prospered', the author of the *Great Chronicle of London* wrote,
'he should have been honourably lauded over all; whereas now
his fame is darkened and dishonoured as far as he was known.'[52]

It is no doubt true that Richard III would not have usurped
the throne and reopened the wars had not the power and prestige
of the monarchy already been weakened by the earlier wars in
which he had been involved and by the earlier usurpation by his
brother. In this sense what happened in 1483–87 is undoubtedly
linked to what happened in 1459–71 and follows from its deeper,
longer-term causes. But beyond that the circumstances and
immediate causes were different. The first wars came as the
culmination of a slowly deteriorating situation in which various
social, economic and political strains put increasing pressure on
royal government. These stresses were likely to have led to
difficulty in the 1450s for any monarch; under Henry VI they
led to civil war and deposition. The second wars came suddenly

and surprisingly after a period of recovery and effective kingship which seemed to have set England on the road to renewed stability. The immediate cause lay less in the incapacity of a king but more in the ambition of a subject. The first wars were the final outcome of a long drawn out and painful collapse of royal authority: the second wars interrupted the process of recovery.

4

THE SCALE OF THE WARS

The wars and English society

Sir Thomas Smith pictured an England in the later-fifteenth century in which the country was running with blood and almost half the population killed. Reaction against such exaggeration has led twentieth-century historians to play down the length of the wars, the level of involvement even in the highest ranks of society and the extent of disruption. Certainly there was a tendency for contemporaries and early historians to dramatise the impact of the wars. But it is possible to go too far in the direction of minimising the scale of the wars. They were not insignificant.

In 1965 J. R. Lander, following W. H. Dunham, confidently asserted that 'during the Wars of the Roses the total period of active campaigning between the first battle of St Albans and the battle of Stoke amounted to little more than twelve or thirteen weeks in thirty-two years'.[1] Lander was rightly taken to task by Anthony Goodman in 1981 who offered his own revised calculation of 'the minimum number of mostly continuous days on which one or more major forces were in arms' of 61 weeks.[2] But even this might be an underestimate. It does of course depend on what one means by 'active campaigning' and 'major forces in arms'. Even so Dr Goodman overlooked several periods when by anyone's definition troops were on the move. He did not include the Lancastrian siege of Yorkist-held Calais between

October 1460 and June 1461 and the associated cross-Channel raiding. Nor did he count the campaigning in Wales between September 1461 and May 1462. More surprisingly he did not take note of the Northumbrian war of March 1463 to June 1464 which saw the battles of Hedgeley Moor and Hexham as well as the final reduction of the castles. And finally one might add Edward IV's abortive march north in August 1470 to suppress FitzHugh's Rising as a period when at least one major force was in arms. It may be that much of this campaigning was taking place on the periphery of the kingdom – Calais and Northumberland – but it was not insignificant. If these campaigns are included the minimum period of military activity on Goodman's basis is doubled to well over two years.

One may wonder, however, whether a state of war is correctly defined merely by the number of days in which forces were actively campaigning. England was at war with France continuously from 1415 to 1444, but it is not certain that military activity took place on every single day of that 30-year period. There is surely a similar sense in which Englishmen were in arms against each other continuously from October 1459 at least until the first reduction of the Northumbrian castles in September 1461, and arguably, if one includes the campaigning in Wales, until the second reduction of the Northumbrian castles at Christmas 1462. Throughout this three-year period there was a state of open if not continuously active war. Similarly between March 1470 and May 1471 there was arguably a state of continuous war. Finally, before leaving the question of the length of time Englishmen were in arms against each other, a distinction needs to be drawn between the two wars. It is indeed the case that the wars of 1483–87 are characterised by only sporadic and short-lived campaigns. On the other hand, between October 1459 and May 1471 Englishmen were in arms, in readiness for war, one against another or actually campaigning during five of eleven and a half years. The first wars were considerably more extensive and long drawn-out than most recent historians have been willing to concede.

A second question related to the length of campaigning is the size of the armies. As Professor Ross pointed out there was in the later-fifteenth century, a propensity to exaggerate the size of the armies that came together to give battle.[3] The numbers fluctuated widely. At St Albans in 1455 there were probably no more than 3,000 on the Yorkist side, 2,000 on the royalist. At Towton, on the other hand, numbers reached their peak. The figure given by the heralds of 28,000 dead is likely to be an exaggeration, but there is common agreement that the battle was fought by large numbers and was particularly bloody. The Lancastrian forces may have been as large as 25,000; the Yorkists, apparently slightly outnumbered, perhaps mustered 20,000 men. No other battle even approached this in terms of numbers engaged. At Barnet, Tewkesbury, Bosworth and Stoke armies are unlikely to have been much larger than 10,000 and could have been smaller.[4]

The precise numbers involved in the various battles will never be known. A more important question is the extent to which the peerage, the political leaders of the realm, was involved in the struggles. This has been a matter of recent dispute. Following K. B. McFarlane's observation that although it was difficult for the heads of the great landed families to hold aloof a surprising number opted to lie low, T. B. Pugh and J. R. Lander argued that after 1461 the majority of the baronage distanced themselves from the dynastic struggle and that, as a whole, the peerage became remarkably indifferent to its outcome. In Lander's calculations whereas approximately 80 per cent of the peers were involved in the fighting in 1460–61, in 1469–71 and 1483–87 the proportion never rose above two-thirds and was frequently as low as one sixth.[5] Charles Ross, however, calculated that at least 70 per cent were engaged in 1469–71, and latterly that there was a similarly high rate of involvement in the battle of Bosworth.[6]

The issue of peerage participation in the wars after 1462 is important for any assessment of their impact on society. For if indeed the majority of the peerage did hold aloof, leaving the issue to be settled by a handful of magnates and members of the rival royal families, it follows that fewer retained gentry and by extension fewer rank and file were drawn in. The fewer the peers involved, the more the wars were divorced from the day-to-day lives of the majority of the men and women of England. In seeking to resolve the issue several general points need to be clarified. First, account has to be taken of peers who could not have been involved because they were children or otherwise incapacitated. A participating ratio has to be of the adult, sane and free peers not of the total number of living barons. Secondly, Pugh and Lander seem to imply that if we do not have cast-iron evidence that a peer was engaged in a particular battle or insurrection then we can deduce that he was indifferent or aloof. This can be doubted on two grounds. One is that our information about who actually fought at a particular battle is not always complete: chroniclers often only noted the names of the dead or the most prominent of the peers. The other is that failure to be at a battle does not necessarily mean aloofness or indifference. Not knowing whether a particular peer fought is not the same as knowing that he was indifferent. Indeed it is extremely difficult to gauge the extent of involvement. As McFarlane pointed out, few rushed headlong into war. There was much to lose. Every battle, every turn of the wheel of fortune, demanded a careful calculation of advantage. It is not surprising therefore that at every stage many were trimmers by conviction or necessity. The two notorious trimmers in 1469–71 were the young John Talbot, earl of Shrewsbury and the older, more experienced Thomas, Lord Stanley. They acted with a circumspection that bordered on deceitfulness, consistently holding back from final commitment to either side and always keeping on good terms with the winners. One might admire their political dexterity or disapprove of their moral flexibility, but aloof and indifferent they were not. Trimming required as much involvement as fighting.

Our problems largely derive from not knowing. Thus five Yorkist peers (the earl of Essex and Lords Audley, Dinham, Dudley and Ferrers) are not named as being present at any engagement in 1469–71. They did enter London in triumph with Edward IV on 21 May 1471, but they could have joined him only after the fighting was done. That they were caught up in the politics of these years is shown by their removal from all commissions during the Readeption.[7] There is therefore a strong presumption that they were known to be favourable towards Edward IV. Two others, Lords Greystoke and Lumley are similarly never named, but they were very much involved in Warwick's northern affinity. If they did not join him and fight at Barnet, it could be that they were stranded in the north, cut off by Henry Percy, the newly restored earl of Northumberland, who by sitting still was judged to have done Edward IV singularly good service. In Northumberland's case neutrality was specifically noted to be effective aid to Edward IV.

Applying the above considerations to the behaviour of the peerage in 1469–71 what do we find? There were approximately 60 peers: approximately because there are one or two problems of definition. Was Edward, Prince of Wales one of the peers? Of this 60, no fewer than 12 (one fifth) were minors, insane or otherwise unavailable (including the fugitive Henry Clifford). Of the remainder, 30 were engaged in one or more battles or risings. Two others, Shrewsbury and Stanley, openly hovered around the action. One John Talbot, Lord Lisle, was killed on an entirely private affair and fourteen or fifteen remain of whom we have no information, including the seven (Essex, Audley, Dudley, Dinham, Ferrers, Greystoke and Lumley referred to above). Whatever else this reveals it does not point to collective indifference or aloofness.

The same consideration can be applied to Bosworth, from which, it has been suggested, most of the barons absented themselves while less than a quarter fought for Richard III. J. R. Lander found that only four were with Henry Tudor. Most recently, Dr Richmond has suggested that only six fought for Richard III and that at least three-quarters of the peerage avoided the field. While Charles Ross was at first willing to go along with these low estimates, in his *Richard III*, placing controversial reliance on the *Ballad of Bosworth Field*, he suggested that no less than twenty peers fought for Richard III.[8] Whether that many did turn out, horsed and harnessed, is impossible to determine. Four were certainly on active service elsewhere: Lords Audley and Dinham; Francis, Viscount Lovell and William Herbert, earl of Pembroke in Calais, southern England and Wales. From subsequent behaviour one can safely deduce that the earl of Lincoln as well as Lords Scrope of Bolton and Masham were there in spirit if not in body. The earl of Shrewsbury, a minor, might or might not have been in the king's custody; his uncle, Sir Gilbert Talbot, however, commanded one wing of Henry Tudor's army. Committed against the king were Jasper Tudor, earl of Pembroke; the earl of Oxford; the marquis of Dorset; Edward Woodville, the new Earl Rivers; Edward Courtenay soon to be created earl of Devon; and, as the event proved, Lord Stanley.

One bedevilling complication in any calculation is that many persons, even if willing and able, may not have had time to reach the field. A particular problem exists with the earl of Northumberland's contingent, raised hurriedly in the north, which might have been expected to include the earl of Westmorland, Lords Fitzhugh, Greystoke, Dacre and Lumley as well as the Scropes. Most, if not all, seem not to have fought. They may not have had time to arrive; or alternatively they may have been present but not engaged.[9] Again failure to engage might have resulted from a deliberate holding back or from being left stranded by the course of the battle. These questions will never be answered. For this reason it is not possible to give a certain answer to the question of who fought for Richard. But failure to fight was not the same as indifference. Similarly it is not possible to say whether or not a number of lords deserted Richard. What is clear is that a majority of the active adult peerage had a stake in the outcome of the trial of strength between Richard III and Henry Tudor in 1485. There is no firm ground for supposing that the majority held aloof.

Where the peers led, the gentry followed. They could not entirely escape involvement. For the very reason that they were not the political leaders, one would not expect as great a proportion of the gentry to be involved. It is even more difficult to identify and impossible to quantify their participation. Occasional lists of casualties and knightings or the record of attainders help, but others are rarely named and many who ended up on the losing side were pardoned or simply allowed to return home untroubled. There is a strong presumption for instance that several of the gentry of north Yorkshire and Cumbria followed Warwick in rebellion in 1469–71 and perhaps fought with him at Barnet. But none of his followers were attainted, and, after 1470, none were required to take out pardons. The reason almost certainly was that Richard, duke of Gloucester quickly took over Warwick's estates, his men and their protection. Warwick himself was not attainted; and neither were his followers.

K. B. McFarlane also argued that although lords retained the service of knights and esquires with the intention that they should follow them in war, in practice they were singularly reluctant to do so. Of course client gentry had the loophole of their allegiance to a crowned king which was almost always written into a contract. On many occasions individual gentlemen made a hard-headed calculation of their personal interest, especially when they faced conflicting loyalties.[10] This is particularly apparent in the case of Henry Vernon of Haddon who found himself importuned in March 1471 by George, duke of Clarence and by Richard Neville, earl of Warwick, both seeking his support. In the event he resolved his dilemma by staying at home.[11] But, as the well-documented histories of the Pastons and Plumptons show, many gentry were not unwilling to follow their lords. This is particularly true of northern England where the Nevilles and Percies, enjoyed the support of loyal and long-serving gentry families.

The senior clergy were more independent. Most bishops owed their appointments to royal favour, but during civil war those who were politically employed (and not all bishops were political creatures) tended to be trimmers. Only a minority became openly partisan. In 1459–61 Thomas Bourchier of Canterbury, William Grey of Ely and George Neville of Exeter were committed Yorkists. In 1470–71 George Neville, now of York, took his brother's part. In 1483 John Morton of Ely, Lionel Woodville of Salisbury and Peter Courtenay of Exeter resisted Richard III. For all these men, with the exception of Morton of aristocratic blood, family loyalties were probably overriding. More typical was John Russell, bishop of Lincoln and Edward IV's last keeper of the privy seal who stayed on to become Richard III's chancellor.[12] Only in Durham where the bishop held extensive temporal authority in the palatinate did the incumbent have no choice but to play a political role. Lawrence Booth (1457–76) is something of an enigma. He was Queen Margaret's confessor before being promoted and came to Durham to curtail the Neville influence which had been built up in the palatinate during the pontificate of his predecessor, Robert Neville. One might have expected Booth to be a stalwart Lancastrian after 1461. Indeed his temporalities were confiscated (and therefore his political power removed) for fifteen months in 1462–64. But subsequently he stood firm for Edward IV during the Readeption and was rewarded with the chancellorship in 1472–74 and promotion to York in 1476. The key to his career, both his disfavour in 1462–64 and favour after 1471, lies almost certainly in a bitter feud with Warwick the Kingmaker and not in a dynastic preference. Booth's successor, William Dudley, was a Yorkist servant who wholeheartedly supported Richard III's usurpation. Unfortunately for the king he died in November 1483. He was succeeded by John Shirwood (1483–91) who spent most of his pontificate in Rome leaving his king a more direct voice in the government of the palatinate. Thus of the bishops of Durham only Booth became fully caught up in political conflict.[13] For the bishops in general, one suspects that, as has recently been suggested, priority was given to maintaining the corporate spirit and solidarity of the English Church in the face of an unstable and unpredictable political world.[14]

No bishop is known to have fought in the wars. The raising of armies and fighting was left to lords and gentry. Troops for civil wars were raised in three principal ways: by deploying the professional soldiers retained for garrison service by the Crown; by calling out household servants and indentured retainers; and by raising the tenantry. Commissions of array, although frequently issued, do not seem often to have contributed to the ranks of actual fighting men in civil war. It is not clear whether levies were always mustered, let alone marched into action. The array was unwilling to leave its own county, and was specifically for defence against a foreign enemy. Thus levies, especially from the northern counties, turned out to fight against the Scots in 1462, 1481 and 1482, but for civil war it seems the commissions are more significant for the names they give of local leaders on whom the king believed he could rely in an emergency, than as evidence that county levies actually responded to a call to arms.

The fewest troops were provided by the garrisons of Carlisle, Berwick (none at all between 1461 and 1482) and Calais. At Carlisle there were barely more than 75 in peace and 150 in war; at Berwick twice that. There is no direct evidence that these soldiers were actually called out by the wardens. They may have remained at their posts in case the Scots took advantage of their absence. The Calais garrison, which was larger, did become involved. Warwick brought a large contingent of the garrison with him to Ludford in 1459. This contingent, under its captain Andrew Trollope, deserted to the queen and served under her command until its defeat at Towton. Despite the desertion of so many of its garrison, Calais was a lifeline to the Yorkists in the winter of 1459–60 and withstood attack from a Lancastrian force. Ten years later the loyalties of the garrison were significant. In the spring of 1470 Warwick was turned away. But in the following year some of the soldiers joined the Bastard of Fauconberg's rising in Kent. Even in 1483, Lord Hastings' threat to call out the garrison helped him carry the day at the crucial council meetings immediately following the death of Edward IV.[15]

Of the two remaining sources of troops, household men and retainers were probably numerically the less significant. This might seem surprising since it has been asserted since the sixteenth century that the late-medieval baronage maintained huge households. In *Utopia* Thomas More put into the mouth of Raphael Hythlodaeus the opinion that there existed in the reign of Henry VII noblemen who carried around with them huge crowds of idle attendants 'wont in sword and buckler to look down with a swaggering face on the whole neighbourhood'. Taken up in the nineteenth century, More's deliberately ambivalent remark led Stubbs to conclude that the baron 'could, if he wished to pay for it, support a vast household of men armed and liveried as servants'. And J. R. Green added that the lord's power lay in the hosts of disorderly retainers who swarmed around their houses, ready to furnish a force in case of revolt. Even as recently as 1965 it has been remarked that baronial retinues reached 'the proportions of small armies' and that greater peers engaged 'considerable numbers of men'.[16]

Closer inspection reveals however that, on the contrary, the manpower thus available to fifteenth-century lords was small. It is difficult to discern the actual size of a noble household let alone the number of armed men maintained in it. In fact the household fluctuated in size. At any one time it would include all manner of people who had just dropped in to pay respects or to take advantage of open house. Thus numbers of meals served is a poor guide. Moreover many household servants were not regularly in attendance or permanently in residence. The *Black Book of Edward IV* laid down the approved sizes of household establishments: a duke was entitled to 240, an earl 140, a baron 40, a knight banneret 24 and a knight bachelor 16.[17] Whether men honoured these quota is impossible to tell. It is known that in 1468 George, duke of Clarence supported 299 persons. Successive dukes of Buckingham kept households of 200–240 between 1440 and 1520. The smaller permanent household, the *domicelli*, of these men is more difficult to gauge. Buckingham's residential staff of yeomen, grooms and pages seems to have numbered 90. These were mainly domestic servants including musicians and chaplains. His itinerant, 'riding' retinue numbered 56 in the year 1439–40. In 1511–12 the fifth earl of Northumberland budgeted for 86 resident personnel out of a total household establishment of 166, of which 55 formed his riding company.[18]

Numbers fluctuated, especially when the lord took to the road, which was frequent. In 1483, according to a surviving household book, John Howard, newly created duke of Norfolk, kept a permanent household of approximately 64 persons. Of these some twenty accompanied him on pilgrimage from his residence at Stoke by Nayland in Suffolk to Walsingham between 16 and 26 August. On 2 September a larger company of 54 went up to London with him, but for a brief visit on 13 September to his estates at Reigate and Horsham Howard took only 20 companions.[19] How many of these men were professional soldiers forming an armed bodyguard is equally hard to say. In the royal household of 500 there was an establishment of 24 yeomen of the Crown, probably in practice 60 or more, veteran archers, who formed the royal bodyguard. In September 1483 Norfolk was accompanied to London by nineteen yeomen who may or may not have formed his bodyguard.[20] The evidence is slight, but what there is clearly does not suggest hordes of armed men swarming around the baronial households.

In time of emergency or on special occasion the lords could, and did, call up their indentured retainers to supplement their households. The maximum number of knights and esquires retained by any lord seems to have been 90; the 90 retained by Lord Hastings after 1471.[21] In the 1440s Humphrey, duke of Buckingham (d.1460) made arrangements for over 80 client gentry to serve him, although only 23 were retained by formal contract. Rarely do contracts specify the number of men that a retainer was to provide 'in time of peace as well as war, horsed and harnessed' at the lord's command. Buckingham was unusually precise in some of his contracts; in these the numbers required from knights and esquires varied between three and six companions per retainer. On this basis Buckingham's formal contracts of retainers were likely only to produce him some 120 men ready for war: hardly a vast army.[22] Some idea of a retinue at full strength, on this occasion ostensibly for peace not war, is provided by the report given by John Bottoner to Sir John Fastolf in January 1458 that Richard Neville, earl of Salisbury descended on London for his reconciliation with the earl of Northumberland accompanied by '400 horse in his company, eighty knights and esquires'; a cryptic report which suggests a body composed of his riding household, 80 retainers and their men.[23] If this interpretation is correct it too suggests only approximately five men in the company of each retainer. This was a retinue at a strength worthy of comment gathered together for a special but politically dangerous occasion, when London was alarmed at the number of armed men descending on it.

When it came to war the participating lords called out their retainers; and were joined by as many as were willing to go. But even at their fullest strength (which was rarely the case), the armed retainers could provide only a nucleus of a lord's company. The numbers were made up by calling out the tenantry. The London chronicler Gregory tells the story of how on the morrow of Blore Heath in 1459, Sir John Dawn's son, hearing of his father's death, promptly raised his tenants and shortly after ambushed Sir John and Sir Thomas Neville (two sons of the earl of Salisbury) and Sir Thomas Harrington near Tarpelay.[24] In the autumn of 1460, when Queen Margaret was gathering her strength for a final confrontation with the Yorkist lords, according to the same authority she wrote to her friends in the west country calling on them to join her as hastily as they could, bringing their tenants 'as strong in their harness as men of war'.[25] In March 1471 Henry Vernon was ordered by Clarence to see that all his and the duke's own tenants and servants were ready upon an hour's notice to serve him. At the same time the earl of Shrewsbury sent warnings to the bailiffs of his Shropshire manors to have his tenants standby.[26] Most clearly documented of all is the case of John Howard, duke of Norfolk who agreed to establish a militia of 1,000 men to serve the king when needed. A muster of February 1484 reveals that he managed to recruit only 800 of which 500 were tenants drawn from 44 manors. A further 180 were promised by 43 named individuals, some of whom can be identified as household men. This was presumably the body of men called out to serve under him at Bosworth.[27] The tenants of lords and their retainers formed the bulk of the armies. Their effectiveness might be questioned: at the second battle of St Albans in March 1461 most of the Lancastrian untrained levies melted away leaving the core of household men and retainers to carry the day.[28] But as far as numbers were concerned armies were primarily composed of tenant militias.

The wars were fought for the most part by the lords, their retainers and above all the tenants of lords and retainers. Wider popular participation was rare. Popular grievances were exploited by dissident magnates to good effect. In 1459–60 the Yorkist lords appealed to the people of Kent and neighbouring counties who had been disillusioned with Lancastrian government since the late 1440s. Their grievances helped give the Yorkists both popular support and much needed credibility in their claim to be pursuing more than factional ends. Similarly in 1469 Warwick and Clarence turned popular disappointment at Edward IV's failure to restore 'good governance' to their own account.[29] But such exploitation of grievances for propaganda and recruitment of support is a far cry from the wars taking on

a popular character. Indeed it is almost certainly the case that
all participants were agreed in their desire *not* to allow conflict
to degenerate into a general uprising. That such a development
was possible is revealed by the fact that from time to time a mob
took a hand in despatching defeated noblemen. In July 1460
Thomas, Lord Scales, who had held the Tower for the court,
was murdered by the Thames watermen after he had been spared
by his fellow peers. One source reports that 'the common people
of the country who loved him not' seized Richard Neville, earl
of Salisbury from Pontefract castle and murdered him after he
had been taken alive at Wakefield. There may well have been
particular local grievances against Salisbury, who had been
steward of the duchy of Lancaster at Pontefract for many years.
In 1468 Humphrey Stafford of Southwick, earl of Devon, in
flight after his defeat at Edgecote was recognised and murdered
by a mob at Bridgwater.[30] Perhaps the nearest the wars came to
involving a popular uprising was when the Bastard of Fauconberg
belatedly raised the people of Kent on the Lancastrian behalf in
May 1471. The rising had much in common with Cade's Revolt
of 1450 and represents in many ways the last eruption of
simmering discontent in the county which had from time to time
become absorbed in the more general conflict. Only in Kent was
wider social conflagration threatened.[31]

The particular experience of Kent reminds us that the wars
had a significant regional dimension. Welsh troops, for instance,
played a prominent role in 1461 when Edward IV raised the
marches. Henry VII drew upon Welshmen in 1485, and the
battle of Edgecote in 1469 was largely a fight between Welsh
and northern levies. Such northern levies were called out
frequently. The men of Richmondshire in particular, where the
Nevilles dominated from Middleham, accompanied Salisbury to
Blore Heath and Ludford in 1459 and were active under the earl
of Warwick in the Northumbrian campaigns of 1461–64. In 1469
they turned out again under the leadership of Robin of Redesdale
and were in arms subsequently in March 1470, August 1470 and
April 1471.[32]

It was perhaps easier for the Nevilles and the Percies and their
local allies to call out the northern tenantry than more southerly

lords to raise theirs because the men of the north were more accustomed to fighting against the Scots. The northern earls enjoyed the services of the garrisons in Carlisle and Berwick. In time of Anglo-Scottish war, these garrisons were augmented by large retinues called out by the retainers of the wardens. Thus in 1448, when war was imminent, Sir Walter Strickland was retained for life by Salisbury. To defend the border Strickland could muster 290 armed tenants (billmen and bowmen, half of them mounted) drawn from 7 manors. In the same war Henry, Lord Fitzhugh rode to Scotland with his tenants of Mickleton in Teesdale (and others no doubt) who were subsequently rewarded for their service.[33] Sheriffs of Yorkshire were accustomed to raising levies to assist in the defence of the marches; the towns of York and Beverley regularly provided contingents; the priory of Durham occasionally sent a company of its 'lay servants' (tenants); and even the archbishop of York on occasion raised a troop of armed clergy.[34] The bishop of Durham, by virtue of his regality, had a more permanent obligation to assist in the defence of the border, not only by raising his own levies but also through his permanent garrison at Norham on Tweed which in time of war in 1482 was established at 30 men.[35]

There was therefore a considerable reservoir of experienced manpower in the northern counties which could be tapped by the rival magnate families, the Nevilles and Percies. One commentator reported that men from the far north played a decisive role in the first battle of St Albans.[36] In 1460–61 it was a largely northern army which Margaret of Anjou led from victory at Wakefield, to St Albans and finally defeat at Towton in 1461. In 1469–70, as we have seen, Warwick made full use of his northern forces in his rebellion against Edward IV. On Edward IV's return in 1471, however, the north was partially neutralised by the king's restoration of the earl of Northumberland and his favour to Bishop Booth of Durham in 1470. Finally in 1483 Richard of Gloucester turned to the north to raise an army to guarantee his usurpation of the throne, while at Bosworth a northern division under Northumberland played a crucial if shadowy role in the outcome.[37]

On one occasion an army from the north ran amok. This was

the army brought down to London by Queen Margaret in the final two months of 1461. It was not just an army of northerners: it contained large contingents recruited in the west country which had marched north to join the queen in December 1460 and also a Scots battalion contributed by the regent, Mary of Guelders. But its bulk was of followers and tenants of the northern lords loyal to the house of Lancaster. As it marched south it cut a swathe of looting and destruction, spreading terror before it.[38] Its behaviour and the fear it created were to have a profound effect on public opinion and attitudes towards the north.

Several chroniclers emphasised the malice and perniciousness of the northerners in 1461. Warwick himself, albeit one who in his time relied heavily on his own northern connections, used the fear of northern rapacity in his propaganda in February 1461. As early as January 1461 the rumour was spreading in Norfolk that the people of the north had been appointed to rob and pillage. After Towton, the political verse *The Rose of Rouen* presented Edward IV as the saviour of the south from the northerners who had threatened to occupy it. Even as late as 1489 Henry VII took up the same theme in his proclamation against the rebels of north Yorkshire whom he painted as intending to 'rob, despoil and destroy' all the south parts of the realm and to bring its people into captivity.[39]

It is hard to tell whether this is mere hysteria cleverly exploited for propaganda purposes, or whether it reveals a truth about north/south divisions. K. B. McFarlane was confident that the wars had no regional dimension; 'these were neither wars between north and south nor between the lowland south-east and the dark corners of the north and west'.[40] In the sense that England was not permanently divided into regional armed camps one cannot disagree. But the northern counties provided a considerable number of the combatants. And while it is undoubtedly true that before 1461 the wars were as much a civil war between the northern earls as between York and the Lancastrian court, after Edward IV came to the throne trouble and disaffection came more exclusively from the north. Warwick used his northern support to harry Edward IV in 1469 and 1470. And Richard III was even more dependent on the same region. This dependence became transparent when, in the aftermath of the widespread rebellion in the southern counties in October 1483, so as to secure his tottering regime he planted many of his northern supporters in the south. It might have seemed that the fear of twenty years earlier had been realised. Moreover after Richard III's fall in 1485 it was indeed the northernmost counties which put up the only sustained resistance to Henry VII.[41] To this extent the kingdom became polarised. The polarisation is reflected in early Tudor writings about Richard III and the north. Even in 1486 the Crowland chronicler could see the north as the source of every evil and Polydore Vergil described the northerners as savage and more eager than others for upheaval.[42] Not without foundation the idea became fixed that Richard III was a northern king who had subdued the south. Thus although one might seriously doubt that the first of the wars were in any meaningful way a conflict between north and south, it would seem that in a very real sense the last wars, the wars of 1483–87 were.

Queen Margaret's march south in the late winter of 1460–61 is the only example of sustained looting and pillaging of the civilian population throughout the wars. Compared with the horrors brought by war to France in the first half of the fifteenth century, England escaped lightly. Philippe de Commynes, a man of affairs knowledgeable about his world, wrote in his memoirs in the 1490s that 'in my opinion, out of all the countries which I have personally known England is the one where public affairs are best conducted and regulated with least damage to the people'.[43] K. B. McFarlane drew attention to the fact that even during the period of most intense military activity and social disruption, June 1460–March 1461, William Worcester could ride freely about England winding up the estate of his master Sir John Fastolf.[44] What new castle building was undertaken, as at Kirby Muxloe by Lord Hastings, was for residential ease not defence. Armies were rarely kept in the field for months on end and towns and castles were not usually besieged for very good cause: lack of resources. It was extremely costly to keep an army on campaign. For this reason more than any other it was imperative for commanders to seek a quick decision. No-one could afford to dig in and fight a war of territorial attrition. Castles, in particular, besides being vulnerable to artillery, were extremely expensive to maintain, man and provision. In so far as many town walls fell into disrepair, they did so for the same reason: the high cost of maintenance in an age of general difficulty in borough finances.[45]

While it is true that for most of the time the wars caused little suffering to most of the people, as Dr Goodman has pointed out the indirect financial effect may have been of greater significance than the apparent lack of physical destruction. Soldiers had to be paid; town watches had to be mounted; farmers downed sickles and went off to war even at harvest time. In 1463–64 neither bishop nor prior of Durham received much revenue from their estates in Northumberland because the county was in the hands of the king's rebels. There were no doubt others who at other times and in other places found the collection of revenues disrupted. Moreover, the prior was probably not alone in finding himself unable to recover a loan made to Queen Margaret in 1461. His bishop too bore the cost of reinforcing the castle and gate on Durham Palace Green when the earls of Westmorland and Northumberland passed through the city on their way to a gathering of Lancastrian troops at Pontefract in 1460.[46] The comparative freedom of England from the worst horrors of war that could be suffered in late medieval Europe, should not lead to the conclusion that the wars had no disruptive effect. Arguably Commynes' comment says more about other kingdoms than about England.

The wars and European politics

As Commynes well knew the Wars of the Roses had an important international dimension. Indeed, from beginning to end political instability and dynastic rivalry were exploited and exacerbated by England's neighbours – France, Scotland and Burgundy. England's weakness provided opportunities for her neighbours to profit at her expense and their security was enhanced by attention to destabilising England. For their part English leaders looked abroad for alliances to strengthen their hands in their internal rivalries. The Wars of the Roses, therefore, became enmeshed in wider European political rivalry.

Before his death in 1460, James II of Scotland made the running in seeking to take advantage of England's internal difficulties. Vainly seeking to put together an international alliance against England, he still went ahead with his own attacks on England in 1455 and 1456. Rebuffed by the duke of York in 1456, James agreed to a truce in 1457. But in July 1460, taking advantage of the civil war, he laid siege to Roxburgh, and, although he was accidently killed when a cannon exploded, the castle was captured. Queen Margaret's plight after Towton, gave the regent Mary of Guelders the opportunity for an even greater coup on 25 April the queen surrendered Berwick in exchange for Scottish aid. For the next three years Lancastrian resistance in Northumberland was sustained by Scottish assistance. In June 1461 Scots as well as Lancastrians attacked Carlisle which Margaret had ceded as well. Edward's response was to ally himself with Scottish dissidents until in 1462 he concluded a truce with the regent. A year later, however, in June 1463 a large-scale Scottish attack in concert with the Lancastrians was launched and Norham was besieged. Edward IV planned a full-scale counterattack, for which he was voted a subsidy by parliament. In the event no major military operation was launched. Indeed a new truce was agreed in December which effectively ended this phase of Anglo-Scottish hostilities.[47] The Scots, however, could be well pleased; they had retaken Roxburgh and Berwick, thus immeasurably strengthening their grip on the border, and had successfully sustained three years of opposition to Edward IV.

Charles VII of France and Philip the Good of Burgundy were less willing than James II of Scotland to take advantage of English divisions at the end of Henry VI's reign. The French and Burgundians only became drawn into English affairs after Edward IV became king. But in 1462, after the accession of Louis XI, Queen Margaret set off to France to seek his support. This was promised in a treaty of alliance sealed at Tours in June. But little that was tangible came of it and in the following

October Louis XI agreed a truce with Edward IV. From 1463 Margaret and her son Edward maintained a Lancastrian court in exile but their prospects became increasingly bleaker until Warwick fell out with Edward IV. Of decisive significance for later developments was the marriage alliance made in 1468 between Edward IV and Charles the Bold, the new and belligerent duke of Burgundy. During the 1460s relationships between Louis XI and his greatest subjects, especially the dukes of Burgundy and Brittany, worsened. The marriage of Margaret of York to Charles the Bold, along with an Anglo-Breton treaty, marked the return of traditional alliance patterns in northern Europe. Nothing came of the triple alliance of 1468 as an anti-French coalition, but it was clear that the lines had been drawn. Thus in 1468 Louis XI supported Lancastrian plots in England, particularly in the form of sponsoring a landing in Wales by Jasper Tudor.[48]

To a significant degree the wars of 1470 and 1471 were the culmination of these diplomatic developments. When Warwick fled from England in 1470 he turned to a Louis XI more than eager to effect a reconciliation between the earl and Queen Margaret and to back the Readeption, the end for which Margaret had been working since 1462. The complete success of this venture not only reopened the dynastic civil war in England but also heralded a European war. Part of the price of Louis' support was England's support in an attack launched in December 1470 on Charles of Burgundy. In February 1471, Warwick honoured his commitment by declaring war on Burgundy. The immediate effect of the declaration of war was to stimulate Charles the Bold into instant backing of an expedition to England under the exiled Edward IV for which he provided 36 ships and a few hundred men. Thus both the Readeption and the restoration of Edward IV were achieved by licence of the rival French princes. Between the summer of 1470 and the spring of 1471 the Wars of the Roses were inextricably bound up with the rivalries and conflicts within the kingdom of France.[49]

After 1471, when Edward IV was at last firmly established on the throne, there was less reason for foreign powers to hope to profit from English divisions. Indeed by taking the initiative and mounting an invasion of France in 1475 Edward IV forced Louis XI back on the defensive. Moreover, by the end of the reign, having fought a successful war against Scotland which in 1482 saw the recovery of Berwick so shamefully surrendered in 1461, Edward IV was in a strong position to dictate terms to his northern neighbours.[50] All was changed by Richard III's usurpation. Although Richard III was able to maintain pressure on the Scots and secure a favourable truce in 1484, he was faced by a kingdom of France once more anxious to exploit England's division for its own advantage. France herself was passing through a minority and rival factions were jockeying for power. It was Henry Tudor's good fortune that when he escaped from Brittany to France in August 1484 he was welcomed by a group anxious to promote his cause. Henry's invasion of England was made with full backing from France. Had he arrived in France any earlier, or delayed any longer, it would not have been forthcoming. As it was the French could justifiably claim, although Henry VII strenuously denied it, that they had made him king of England, their gain being a five-year respite from English hostility.[51]

What was sauce for the goose in 1485 was sauce for the gander thereafter. Margaret of Burgundy gave whatever backing she could to the successive Yorkist pretenders to the English throne. Perkin Warbeck, the more successful by gaining both Scottish and Burgundian support, became in the 1490s a significant thorn in Henry VII's side. Thus the wars were not only sustained, but also extended by the intervention of foreign powers. A major principle of international diplomacy in the late-fifteenth century was the destabilisation of rival powers by whatever means lay at hand. Thus support was almost always given to pretenders or dissidents. It was a policy followed as much by English as by Scottish and French kings. But by their intervention in the Wars of the Roses the foreign powers successfully made matters significantly worse in England than they would otherwise have been.

In the scale of fighting, the extent to which they involved and divided Englishmen, in their domestic impact and their frequent exacerbation by foreign intervention, the Wars of the Roses were more grave than some recent commentators have been willing to recognise. Perhaps there has been a tendency to play them down because of a failure to distinguish clearly enough between the scale and character of the different wars themselves. The first wars, the wars between Lancaster and York of 1459 to 1471, were by any reckoning major civil wars: they included the longest continuous period of civil war in English history between the reign of King Stephen and the English Civil War in the seventeenth century. They may not have caused as much physical destruction and loss of life as full-scale international war in fifteenth-century Europe and they may have been less totally disruptive of English society than the civil wars of the seventeenth century. But they were a major breakdown of normal political life: in one way or another they involved the greater part of the political nation. Moreover, as a result of usurpation and dynastic conflict, both wars significantly weakened the standing of the English monarchy. The throne changed hands violently 5 times in under 25 years. By 1484 the English had earned the unenviable reputation abroad of killers of kings. The major legacy of the wars was the damage they had inflicted on royal authority. The major task of reconstruction was the restoration of that authority.

5

AFTERMATH AND THE WIDER CONTEXT OF THE WARS

The restoration of royal authority

Just as nineteenth-century historians, following sixteenth-century writers, saw the Wars of the Roses in terms of uncontrolled anarchy so also they painted a dramatic picture of their consequences. In short, during the wars the old feudal baronage dashed itself to pieces and out of them emerged a 'New Monarchy', despotic in character, founded on the support of the landed and commercial middle classes.[1] Little of this account has stood the test of modern scholarship. It is clear now that the old feudal baronage did not commit collective suicide; no middle class emerged to take its place; and although royal authority recovered and was enhanced, few would now describe early Tudor monarchy as 'new'. Just as the wars themselves were not so dire, so also the changes they wrought were not so sweeping.

The idea that the ancient nobility of the land was destroyed has early antecedents and was a tale that grew in the telling. Thomas More in his *History of King Richard III* remarked that so great was the bloodshed that scarcely half of the ancient noble blood of the realm remained. His contemporary William Tyndale was prepared to go so far as to assert that only one sixteenth remained: 'their own sword hath eaten them up'. Towards the end of Elizabeth I's reign Sir Thomas Craig drew attention to the destruction of the royal house by making use of 'a Scripture phrase': 'there was not one left to piss against the wall'.[2] Craig was broadly correct about the royal blood of Edward III. Eventually, and as much as a consequence of the relentless pursuit of rivals by Henry VII and Henry VIII as of the accident of war, all the remaining blood royal was concentrated in the veins of the Tudors and Stuarts. But the other ancient noble families did not destroy themselves. K. B. McFarlane convincingly demonstrated that throughout the late Middle Ages there was a natural rate of attrition in the ranks of the peerage at an average of 25 per cent per quarter century and a constant replenishing by new families. In fact between 1450 and 1500 the failure rate was slightly lower than average. Thirty-eight noble families outside the royal family, failed in the male line in this half century, twelve by violent means. But of that twelve, seven were already doomed in the male line; that is the man killed had no male children and no likelihood of fathering them. Thus Richard Neville, earl of Warwick had only two girls. When he died his countess was 46 and she lived for a further 21 years. On the other hand innumerable sons of Percy were killed, yet the family was fertile enough to survive. The one ancient family destroyed in the direct male line was, he argued, that of Courtenay and even that survived in a collateral branch.[3] Indeed the same is true of the Nevilles, for although the kingmaker himself had only two daughters, a part of his inheritance was entailed and should have descended to his cousin, Richard Neville, Lord Latimer.

If in the end only a handful at most of noble families were extinguished by the wars, the wealth and power of some were severely curtailed by attainder and forfeiture. The Hungerford family, for instance, was ruined and was not able to recover financially until the 1530s.[4] Many families suffered attainder and forfeiture and, although reversal was frequent (64 per cent of all those attainted between 1453 and 1504, as much as 84 per cent of the peerage, were ultimately restored), the delays and costs involved in recovering lands in the meantime granted elsewhere meant that many compounded with the beneficiaries and accepted only partial recovery. Although the penalties of defeat and proscription were ultimately lifted on all but a handful of noble families, the permanent loss was greater than the mere fact of restoration suggests. In this respect several lords suffered a diminution of wealth and power.[5]

More important than actual loss of lands and income was the political leverage which attainder and forfeiture gave a king. Not only could the hope of restoration provide an effective incentive for good service (as it did with Thomas Howard, earl of Surrey after 1485), but also the fear of loss of confiscated estates could similarly ensure continued loyalty from a beneficiary. Henry VII proved himself particularly adept at exploiting the power this gave him over both his erstwhile opponents and his own supporters. Although it is possible that after 1485 there was a change in the mood of the old nobility; that, especially after the shocks of Richard III's usurpation, they became politically more circumspect or even craven,[6] it is more likely that nobles were more subservient because they were subjected to a more effective deployment of royal authority.

The recovery of royal authority has been credited not just to Henry VII but additionally to Edward IV, who after 1471 supposedly laid the foundations of a new monarchy. Much depends on what is meant by a new monarchy. If by this phrase one merely understands that kings were obeyed then certainly Edward IV in his latter years meets the requirement. But this still begs the question as to whether Edward's approach and means were novel, or indeed whether they were far-sighted in terms of a perceived objective of establishing royal authority on a new, stronger and more permanent basis. This is to be doubted.

At the heart of the idea of a new monarchy is an emphasis on administration. It is the development of household government, of regional and specialist councils, and of chamber finance which gives it its special characteristic. The key lies in the royal household, for Edward IV, Richard III and Henry VII preferred to act directly through their household officers and servants, especially their secretaries and treasurers of the household, rather than through the established departments of state, chancery and treasury, which had lost importance under Henry VI and during the earlier wars. There is little doubt that such an approach gave more direct and effective control. Since the restoration of royal solvency was a necessary precondition of effective government, the system of chamber finance developed by Edward IV and perfected by Henry VII was of major significance. The king, as Sir John Fortescue pointed out, needed to be considerably more wealthy than any of his subjects. Chamber finance, by cutting down on bureaucracy and by giving more direct and immediate control to the king, was one means by which this was achieved.[7]

However, the importance and significance of the administrative practices adopted by Edward IV and his successors can be exaggerated and misunderstood. Not everything was brought into the household. Chancery and exchequer continued to shoulder a share of the administrative burden. Secondly, although revenues increased dramatically – to £60,000 per annum at the end of Edward IV's reign, reaching £110,000 after 1500 – not all of the increase was the product of administrative zeal. Some from customs and excise was the result of expanding international trade. The royal demesne was extended by the acquisition of new estates – especially those of York and Warwick – by usurpation, by resumption and by forfeiture. While Edward IV tended to grant out the royal demesne for political patronage rather than retain it for financial gain, Henry VII kept most of the land in hand. Moreover, between 1471 and 1509 there was a general rise in rents as a result of a resurgent demand for land. Thus the income from Crown land quadrupled from £10,000 per annum at the end of Edward IV's reign to over £40,000 per annum at the end of Henry's, more as a result of a change of policy and changing economic circumstance than as a consequence of administrative organisation.[8] But perhaps the most important reason for Henry's spectacular financial success was the avoidance of costly foreign adventures. Edward IV avoided war after 1471 more by mischance than judgement: Henry VII followed a foreign policy carefully constructed to keep out of war if at all possible. Peace abroad allowed financial entrenchment at home. As Henry VIII was rapidly to discover, the revenues available to the Crown were quite inadequate for the support of a sustained war on the continent of Europe.

Furthermore the development of household administration was neither novel nor necessarily a step forward. A tendency towards bringing administration back into the household can be traced back to the reign of Richard II.[9] Then attempts to bypass the offices of state before 1386 and after 1396 aroused fierce opposition. It is one of the ironies of history that what Richard II attempted in his reign has been roundly condemned while the Yorkist revival of the same has been widely praised. No doubt the circumstances were different, but clearly household government was not entirely new. Indeed household government was essentially factional in genesis. It is arguable that it was reintroduced by Margaret of Anjou when she gained control of the government in 1458.[10] Chamber finance began as the expedient of victorious factions. Even after 1471 Edward IV's regime retained some of this quality, for the royal household was the organised body of the king's servants and friends. To fall back on a partisan household in time of civil war no doubt made eminent political sense, but in truth it was a retreat from the more public bureaucratic style of government practised by earlier kings in more settled times.[11]

In fact, in the last resort, the primary significance of household government was political not administrative. And it is in this political dimension that Henry VII differed most markedly from Edward IV. Edward IV's household was dominated by his kinsmen and close friends, all great lords. His rule in the country was to a large degree exercised by them assisted by his knights and esquires of the body. Edward IV established a regime founded on regional authority delegated to his most trusted lieutenants. In the far north and the north-east he relied on his brother, Richard of Gloucester; in Lancashire and Cheshire on Thomas, Lord Stanley; in the north midlands on Lord Hastings; in Wales and the marches on Earl Rivers; and in the west midlands and south-west on his brother, George of Clarence, until 1477 and thereafter Thomas Grey, marquis of Dorset. The south-east was more directly under the sway of himself and lesser household men. These magnates and their powerful affinities were allowed a large degree of autonomy. Supervision of the local administration of justice was left largely to them: the king's concern was 'to make things hold still'. Like Charles II two centuries later, his priority was to avoid going on his travels

again. Thus security took precedence over all else. This meant
that the administration of justice locally tended to be partial.
Where his deputy chose, as did Richard of Gloucester in the
north, to attempt to provide impartial rule the effect was
beneficial and the regime popular. The frequency with which
disputes were referred to and settled by baronial councils such
as Gloucester's reflects the extent to which the king allowed his
men to take over. Only when incompetence, naked self-interest
or quarrelling within the ranks of his household threatened to
disrupt the peace did the king step in.[12]

Far from attacking the power of mighty subjects at its root,
Edward IV sought to channel it towards his own advantage. He
relied heavily on his own personal authority over his kinsmen
and servants and on their own committed loyalty to him. In a
sense the regime was a form of royally sponsored bastard
feudalism. Its antecedents were feudal; its cultural connotations
Arthurian. It was profoundly backward looking, the very anti-
thesis of new monarchy. While Edward lived it worked. It was
however an expression of his weakness not his strength: the
consequence of his dependence on a small but powerful section
of the political élite. After his death its disintegration was rapid.

Henry VII followed a different path. To an extent he had no
choice. Unlike Edward IV or Richard III he did not come to
the throne at the head of a powerful indigenous affinity. He led
an ill-matched coalition of die-hard Lancastrians and excluded
Edwardian Yorkists. He was the adopted head of the remnant
of Edward IV's household, not its long-established leader.
However, because they were exiled and proscribed, for many of
his supporters restoration was ample reward. Thus Edward
Courtenay, the new earl of Devon; John de Vere, earl of Oxford;
Jasper Tudor, earl of Pembroke and Edward Woodville, the new
Earl Rivers did not have to be rewarded beyond the recovery of
their titles, estates and local eminence. Moreover Henry had no
royal family to satisfy other than his childless uncle, Jasper.
What was in one respect a weakness, Henry made a strength,
for he deliberately turned his back on the creation of new mighty
subjects. His treatment of the marquis of Dorset, his queen's
half-brother is revealing. Dorset, like his mother Elizabeth

Woodville, had sought to make his peace with Richard III in 1484. For this reason Henry never trusted him. He was put into prison in 1487 during Lambert Simnel's rising and in 1492 Dorset entered into a humiliating contract with the king whereby he agreed to find sureties and remain loyal in exchange for a royal pardon and admission to the king's favour. He was made to transfer all his lands bar two manors to trustees who were to hold them for the king and to find a recognisance of £10,000.[13] By such means potentially unreliable mighty subjects were reduced to impotence.

Henry did not exclude or neglect his peers. They continued to play an important ceremonial role and two-thirds are known to have attended the royal council. But he allowed their numbers to dwindle by 30 per cent and kept them constantly under pressure whether it was through recognisances and bonds, the promise (or threat) of restoration, the strict licencing of retaining or the enforcement of the Crown's feudal rights. Breaches of the laws against retaining, which the king tightened to give himself more effective control, were ruthlessly punished. Thus the earls of Oxford and Devon as well as Lord Abergavenny were fined heavily and placed under substantial recognisances for flouting the laws.[14] Similarly the king exploited to the full his feudal rights over tenants-in-chief. In the mid-1490s a series of commissions were set up to uncover concealments. When lords failed to follow the correct procedures they were promptly fined. Katherine, dowager duchess of Buckingham was fined for remarrying without the king's licence in 1496 and her son Edward, the duke himself, for entering his inheritance in 1498 without licence before he was 21. The duke subsequently claimed that these had cost him over £7,000. Henry, fifth earl of Northumberland was fined £10,000 in 1505 for abducting an heiress: that is claiming as his own ward the heiress of Sir John Hastings of Fenwick whom the king asserted was his own tenant-in-chief.[15] The peers, particularly the magnates, were as vulnerable, perhaps more vulnerable, than lesser landowners to Henry's heavy lordship.

While Henry used every means at his disposal to reduce the pretensions of mighty subjects he also did his utmost to build up his own power. The restoration of royal finances was a key element in this. The king recognised the truth of Fortescue's analysis that the secret of recovering royal authority lay in making himself richer than his subjects. This was one reason why, unlike Edward IV, he retained possession of the Crown lands. But there was another reason. Land was the basis of local power. By keeping royal estates in hand and administering them locally through his own household servants Henry maintained a direct presence throughout his kingdom.[16] This factor was perhaps most significant in the north of England where Henry VI and Edward IV had enjoyed very little direct control. In so far as Richard III had drawn his strength from the north and the most sustained opposition to Henry in his early years came from that region, it was imperative that he should secure control. By inheriting Richard III's personal estate in the region, as well as recovering his earldom of Richmond, he had the advantage over Edward IV of a substantial landed presence in the North Riding of Yorkshire and County Durham. He could have restored either Ralph Neville, earl of Westmorland or Richard Neville, lord Latimer to the one-time Neville estates held by Richard III. Characteristically he chose to keep them. He had succeeded by conquest to the position of the mightiest northern subject of the preceding 30 years and had no intention of relinquishing that advantage.

The old Neville and duchy of Lancaster lordships were the foundation of a royal presence in the north which had been absent before 1483. Although Henry did not at first continue with Richard III's expedient of a council in the north, he did draw, like his predecessor, on the resources and manpower of those estates. But he also brought in his own household servants – men like Sir William Tyler, Sir Richard Cholmondley and Richard Fox, bishop of Durham (1494–1501) – to act as his agents. Neither could he, nor did he wish to dispense with the services of the local peerage – notably the earl of Northumberland. Nevertheless he made it clear to both Northumberland and the earl of Westmorland, both imprisoned for a brief while after Bosworth, that they were his servants not his masters. After the fortuitous death of Northumberland in 1489, the earl of Surrey, partially restored and totally dependent on the king, was sent north as his unofficial lieutenant. Only in 1501, after Fox and Surrey were recalled to the Court, was a council in the north reconstituted under the presidency of Thomas Savage, archbishop of York. Whether acting through his household servants, peers or senior clergy Henry enforced his own personal authority on the north.[17] In this respect he continued what Richard III had instituted. But in the north of England, on the basis of his own landed estate, he effected a major change of policy and removed one of the primary causes of political instability.[18]

Central supervision of government and a constant watch on all his subjects were the hallmarks of Henry's reign. Whether personally or through council the king kept his finger on the pulse and let little pass unnoticed. Thus, to take a routine example, in 1499 the king himself examined the indentures of Sir Richard Cholmondley and Sir Thomas Darcy as border commissioners, and, as Richard Fox (keeper of the privy seal responsible for completing them) reported, 'at the sight thereof hath found divers and many things therein that he hath caused to be amended'.[19] The king maintained a direct oversight over everyday matters of government. He also kept a keen watch on his own servants. Lord Daubeney was fined for embezzlement of the Calais garrison wages. Sir Richard Empson was not able to slip through an appointment to office for life but saw the king amend the grant to 'during pleasure'.[20] As Dr Davies expressed it, Henry employed 'a nicely judged lack of generosity in dealing with his supporters'.[21] Everyone, friend and foe alike, felt the force of Henry's rule.

Henry VII was not as ruthless, consistent or as continuously successful as this brief account implies. He faced major rebellions, especially in 1497, and was never entirely secure on the throne. But by ceaseless vigilance and unrelenting pressure on all his subjects, great and small, he made himself respected, feared and obeyed. His policy represented a major departure from the policy of Edward IV. By it he began again the process of clawing back lost regality.

The recovery of royal authority after the Wars of the Roses was personal not institutional. For the most part the policies and practices followed by Henry VII were traditional and had been tried before. Richard II had attempted to revert to household government. Henry V had used similar devices to assert his authority over his mighty subjects. Henry VII followed with more lasting success in the footsteps of earlier kings. It has been argued recently that he took personal control to a new level and thus set up a pattern of supervisory and interventionary kingship which was to be the hallmark of Tudor monarchy.[22] In so far as Henry VII successfully reasserted royal control over mighty subjects, controlled the abuses of retaining, made the government of the localities answerable once more to the Crown and reimposed his feudal rights he tackled the long-term roots of the Wars of the Roses which stretched back to the reign of Edward III. But England at the end of his reign was not socially or constitutionally a different kingdom from England in the middle of the fourteenth century. There was no certainty that what he had achieved would not die with him. The joyous accession of Henry VIII demonstrated that he had successfully established a new dynasty, but the new king's early acts suggested that there was not necessarily a new dynastic style of kingship. On coming to the throne Henry VIII abandoned his father's methods of close personal supervision of government, instituted an aristocratic revival and, above all, immediately embarked on a traditional foreign policy of aggression towards France. In his first years Henry VIII revealed all the characteristics of an old-style English king secure on his throne. His confidence and behaviour may have demonstrated that the Wars of the Roses were effectively over, but they did not suggest that England was embarked on a new course. That Henry VII's style of kingship subsequently became the hallmark of sixteenth-century monarchy was due to a succession of able ministers who carried his torch and the impact of new forces which began to transform the kingdom later in Henry VIII's reign and to wrench it into a new and unfamiliar world.

England's neighbours

Henry VIII's brief and inglorious revival of the Hundred Years'

War is a reminder that England at the end of the fifteenth century was still part of a feudal European society. In the political world of the kingdoms of the Atlantic seaboard, civil war such as the Wars of the Roses was the rule not the exception. Extended periods of internal strife, in some kingdoms involving dynastic as well as factional struggle, were characteristic not only of England, but also of Scotland, Aragon, Castile and France. All these kingdoms were prone to similar strains and everywhere the maintenance of domestic peace was precarious because it depended on the capacity of an individual hereditary monarch personally to hold together a fragmented and decentralised polity with severely limited resources, negligible armed force and skeletal bureaucracies at his disposal. The Wars of the Roses were not a uniquely English phenomenon: 'inward war' was the common experience of the kingdoms of Western Europe in the later-fifteenth century. The wars need to be seen in this wider contemporary context.

For England's closest neighbour, Scotland, the fifteenth century has long been a byword for conflict, murder and civil war. Recently, however, as with England, the interpretation of its fifteenth-century history has been substantially revised.[23] Scotland was a tiny kingdom. Its population of some 400,000 was but a sixth of that of England and minute compared with France. In a polity in which the royal revenues rarely surpassed £8,000 per annum and in which the king had to rely utterly on the willing cooperation of his greater subjects for the administration of justice and the defence of the realm, it was intensely critical that the king enjoyed good relationships with them. The earls, lords and lairds of Scotland enjoyed a degree of local autonomy not found south of the border. In many ways the king presided over a federation. When one also bears in mind that in the fifteenth century every king came to the throne as a child and that there were more than 40 years of minority or conciliar rule, it is not surprising that successive kings found it difficult to assert their authority. Two met violent deaths at the hands of their own subjects: James I was assassinated in 1437 and James III killed in battle in 1488.

Yet, if personally unattractive, successive Stewart kings –

James I, James II and James III, were in their different ways effective rulers. While all faced plots and rebellions – especially James II in dealing with the Douglases in 1450–55, James III in coping with his disgruntled brother the duke of Albany in 1479–84 and finally in the baronial revolt which led to his death at Sauchieburn – never did the whole kingdom slide into sustained civil war. Recently James III's career and reign have been likened to that of Richard III; but in many ways that unfortunate king was more like Richard II. Moreover, although two kings were killed (James I and James III), both were succeeded without challenge by their heirs.[24] For all its weaknesses the Scottish monarchy, indeed the kingdom as a whole, had a greater resilience than England. If a comparison in Scottish medieval history is to be drawn with the English Wars of the Roses it lies in the civil war between Bruce and Balliol in the first half of the fourteenth century which was overtaken by English intervention. Indeed it has been plausibly suggested that the memory of the Wars of Independence acted as a powerful restraint on Scottish kings and nobles of the fifteenth century who were only too conscious of the advantage the English might take of their own internal divisions.[25]

In many ways the kingdom of France was like the kingdom of Scotland only on a grander scale. It too was fragmented and decentralised. The king exercised direct control over only a small part of his vast kingdom. Most of it was ruled by appanaged princes who enjoyed considerable legal, financial and military autonomy. These included not only the duchies of Acquitaine (until 1453), Brittany (until 1491) and Burgundy (the duchy itself until 1477), but also others such as Anjou, Bourbon, Orleans and Navarre. As in Scotland the effective enforcement of royal authority depended to a large extent on the mystique of kingship and personal competence.[26] But perhaps because the kingdom was so much larger and the great subjects so much more powerful, France was more prone to civil war.

France's misfortunes during the fifteenth century, so much greater than either England or Scotland, stemmed to a considerable degree from the madness of Charles VI who, after 30 years of insanity, died in 1422. Rivalry for control of the kingdom between factions headed by the dukes of Burgundy on the one hand and the dukes of Armagnac and Orleans on the other led in 1410 to intermittent civil war which lasted until 1435. This internal strife was compounded by the intervention of Henry V of England. On one level Henry V acted as a French subject, for he was duke of Acquitaine and successfully recovered in 1417–19 possession of the duchy of Normandy. But Henry V also revived the Plantagenet claim to the throne of France and was adopted as heir in 1420 while his son was crowned king in 1431. Henry V transformed a civil war into a dynastic conflict, for he was from 1420 the candidate of the Burgundian faction which fought with fluctuating enthusiasm for his cause for fifteen years. From a French point of view the wars of 1420–35 were a struggle between rival parties for the throne itself. Only after the rapprochement between Burgundy and the Valois king, Charles VII, did the struggle unequivocally take on the character of a war to rid the kingdom of the English.[27]

After the final expulsion of the English from Normandy in 1450 and Acquitaine in 1453 the problem of Burgundy still remained. Although the conglomerate of duchies, counties and lordships held by the Valois duke of Burgundy in the Netherlands and eastern France have been described as a state, they never acquired the coherence, autonomy or status of a separate kingdom. In the last resort the duke of Burgundy was a subject of the king of France in Flanders, Artois, Picardy and the duchy of Burgundy as well as of the Empire in the county of Burgundy and his other dominions. The ambition of the dukes of Burgundy, especially Charles the Bold, effective ruler from 1464 to 1477, ensured the periodic revival of civil war in France. In 1465 Louis XI faced an alliance of dissident princes led by Charles calling themselves the League of the Public Weal. The climax of several months of civil war was the bloody battle of Monthéry which left Burgundy with the advantage. Fighting between Louis XI and Charles the Bold was renewed in 1471, 1472 and 1475 but it was not until after the duke's death in January 1477 that Louis launched an all-out assault on his French territories. The duchy of Burgundy was rapidly overrun and subsequently retained. All-out war between Louis and Maximilian of Austria, the regent of the Burgundian inheritance, relieved by two truces in 1478–79 and 1480–81, lasted until a treaty of peace was agreed in December 1482 by which Artois as well as the duchy of Burgundy was to be ceded to France.[28]

After the death of Louis XI in 1483, during the minority of Charles VIII, matters were compounded by renewed factional conflict at Court between the regent Anne of Beaujeu (the king's aunt) and Louis, duke of Orleans (the heir presumptive) and by the crisis of the Breton succession. The government of Anne of Beaujeu faced conspiracies and rebellions of dissident lords inspired by Louis of Orleans until he was taken prisoner at the battle of Saint-Aubin-du-Cormier in 1488. The objective of the government in Brittany was to integrate the duchy more fully into the kingdom either by force or by marriage treaty. It faced determined opposition from a powerful group of Breton nobles. The Breton war which began in 1487 and continued, with a brief interlude in the latter months of 1488, until 1491 coalesced with the Orleanist and Burgundian conflict. Maximilian of Austria revoked the treaty of Arras and joined Breton and other enemies of Anne of Beaujeu in 1487, 1488 and 1490–91. At the same time Maximilian himself faced revolt from the cities of Flanders, for a time being held captive by the Brugeois in 1488, and the French government intervened in Flanders to sustain and support the rebels. Civil strife was as severe in France in the 1480s as in any other western European kingdom in the second half of the fifteenth century. It was ended in 1491 when Charles VIII restored Orleans to favour and, later in the year, married Anne of Brittany. In 1493 the Burgundian war was brought to a similar end by the treaty of Senlis in which Artois and other lordships were restored to Burgundy on the condition that the young Duke Philip do homage. Thus, in the early 1490s a period of French civil war was brought to an end only on the eve of, and to prepare the ground for, Charles VIII's invasion of Italy.[29]

In Spain matters were similarly unsettled.[30] Spain comprised three kingdoms: Aragon, Castile and Portugal, two of which (Aragon and Castile) later united to form the kingdom of Spain. Both Aragon and Castile were wracked by civil war in the second half of the fifteenth century. Aragon, based on Catalan commercial wealth, was a leading Mediterranean power. But between 1462 and 1472 it was reduced to impotence by civil war which culminated in the siege of Barcelona. The war combined elements of a popular revolt and a conflict between the old contractual traditions of Catalonia and a new drive towards absolutism introduced by the king, Juan II. In neighbouring Castile, a kingdom recently carved out of the reconquest of central Spain from the Moors, absolute authority was already well established. Nevertheless this kingdom too was plunged into civil war between 1460 and 1480. The first civil war (1464–74) resulted largely from the incompetence of the king Enrico IV (d.1474), called the impotent because of the later slur that he could not possibly have fathered his daughter Juana. Enrico was in some respects not unlike Henry VI of England and under his slack rule factional rivalry slid into open war. In 1465 his enemies deposed him in effigy and attempted, unsuccessfully, to replace him by his child brother Alfonso (d.1468). When Enrico died in 1474 he left a disputed succession between his only surviving daughter Juana and his half-sister Isabella who had already married Ferdinand, the new king of Aragon. Between 1475 and 1477 they fought and defeated the supporters of Juana to secure control of Castile and fought off Portuguese intervention. By 1480 Isabella and Ferdinand were triumphant.

The history of the civil wars in Castile is further reminiscent of the Wars of the Roses in the manner in which subsequently Isabella, the victor, was presented as the saviour of her kingdom; the one who had rescued it from anarchy. Moreover, in order to justify her disputed succession, the reputation of the unfortunate Enrico II was blackened to much the same effect as was Richard III blackened by Henry VII.[31] As in England, however, it is debatable whether the civil wars were as destructive or the previous kings as disastrous as the victor claimed. The fact is that the Catholic monarchs, Ferdinand and Isabella, went on to achieve the expulsion of the Moors from Granada, the unification of their kingdoms and the conquest of the Americas. It was in their 'Golden Age' that the foundations of Spain's future greatness were laid. Their later success, like the Tudors, vindicated their dubious rise to power.

The late medieval monarchies of Europe were fundamentally fragile and prone to civil disorder. Political stability and harmony depended ultimately on the personal capacity of individual kings. In the second half of the fifteenth century the western kingdoms all endured upheaval and civil war as a result of disputed, ineffective or overbearing rule. The Wars of the Roses in England were by no means unique. They were part of a common experience before a general revival of monarchical authority which took place at the end of the century. The disorder and political instability suffered by England during the Wars of the Roses was comparable with the instability suffered by neighbouring kingdoms. This fact did not escape Philippe de Commynes who, after giving a brief account of the Wars of the Roses, commented that God sets up enemies for princes who forget whence their fortunes come as 'you have seen and see every day in England, Burgundy and other places'.[32]

CONCLUSION

A central feature of this study has been the thesis that there were two Wars of the Roses of contrasting characters: the wars between Lancaster and York of 1459–71 and the wars between York and Tudor of 1483–87. The second of these wars were much as recent historians have described the wars as a whole: a sporadic succession of executions, rebellions and occasional battles. The first, however, involved in two separate phases periods of sustained fighting and complete disruption of normal political life. By any reckoning, in terms of the scale, length and degree of involvement of the political nation, they were major civil wars. It is possible to trace deep-rooted causes relating to developments in government and society stretching back for a century. The nature of these deep-rooted causes has traditionally been misunderstood and their importance exaggerated. It was not bastard feudalism and the retaining of baronial armies as such which led inevitably to the Wars of the Roses. Bastard feudalism was but a form of the customary working of patronage in a patriarchal society. It did not spawn hordes of retainers with nothing to do but brawl and fight each other. The longer-term causes of the wars of Lancaster and York lay rather in a shift in the balance of power between Crown and mighty subject of which the excesses of retaining were a symptom not a cause. By the mid-fifteenth century what was anyway always a precarious balance difficult for the Crown to maintain had been tilted marginally but significantly against the Crown. This was not itself enough to cause the breakdown of civil order. Matters were aggravated by economic depression, financial stress and defeat abroad. Civil war ultimately occurred because of the utter unfitness of Henry VI to rule. A competent king would have faced difficulties after 1450: a physically and mentally weak king was overwhelmed.

While not creating the 'very chaos' pictured by Sir Thomas Smith, the first wars were the most serious civil wars to afflict England between the twelfth and seventeenth centuries. The second wars were less socially disruptive. But paradoxically, in the rapid changes of regime between 1483 and 1485 they may have more seriously weakened the prestige of the Crown than the events of 1459–71. It was then too that polarisation between north and south briefly threatened to become a deeper regional division within the realm. Yet, both in terms of past English experience and in terms of contemporary European experience, these wars were unexceptional in their character. The kingdoms of the west were generally prone to such conflict and instability. Civil war was a more frequent experience of late-medieval than of modern societies. Indeed one might wonder whether the Wars of the Roses have taken on such a distinctive and dramatic image in English history because, whatever their scale, they proved to be the last of such characteristic medieval civil upheavals. It is tempting to think that civil wars of their kind ceased because the monarchy became more powerful, more centralised and more institutionalised and thereby less dependent on the personal qualities of a particular king. It is tempting, but probably wrong. However much it may be debated whether Henry VII or Thomas Cromwell was the architect of a distinctive Tudor government, the power of the kings of England nevertheless still remained rudimentary, fragile and ultimately dependent on the assent and cooperation of their subjects. The Tudors were skilled at adapting and improving the existing machinery. Tudor administrators made the established system of mixed monarchy work. However, as the events of the seventeenth century were to show, it was still possible for the system to break down.

Perhaps the crucial change in the sixteenth century lay not in what was achieved by, but in what was expected of, royal government. A more ordered, stable political society came to be desired by subjects as much as by kings. In the light of rising expectations of civil order, what had happened in the later-fifteenth century came to be viewed with increasing distaste. The sixteenth-century myth of the Wars of the Roses drew its lasting strength not from the persuasiveness of royal propaganda but from a more fundamental change of attitude. There was a genuine fear in Elizabethan England that the kind of civil war experienced before 1487 could happen again. The fear related not so much to what really had happened then as to what was believed could occur 100 years later. It existed because Elizabethans accepted that the Crown had an overriding duty to maintain order, dispense impartial justice and secure internal peace against all disrupters great as well as small. Herein lies the force of Edward Hall's claim that while all other divisions and discords flourished, the root cause of disunity, royal impotence, had been removed. Dynastic division itself may not have been the fundamental cause, but the idea of the warring roses neatly symbolised the new opinion that there was a unity and supremacy to royalty which was not to be challenged. Thus while the Wars of the Roses were not literally the revival of 'sackage, carnage and wreckage', the fact that they were portrayed as such is almost as important. In an era of changing political attitudes, they signified an extreme of disobedience, rebellion and anarchy which was no longer tolerable. The Wars of the Roses stood for a degree of political disorder which had become unacceptable and thus represented the hope and desire for a different present. The change in perceptions and expectations about how politics should be conducted and ordered explains why the immediate past was painted in such lurid colours. It is in the realm of political attitudes rather than of political behaviour that the Wars of the Roses represent a turning point in English history. Their end marked the beginning of that modern attitude which deplores the pursuit of political ends by force.

REFERENCES

INTRODUCTION

1. *The Sunday Times*, 17 July 1977.
2. R. H. Wells, *Shakespeare, Politics and the State* (London: Macmillan, 1986), p. 7.
3. W. C. Sellar and R. J. Yeatman, *1066 and all that*, second ed. (London: Methuen, 1975), p. 54.
4. A. Goodman, *The Wars of the Roses: Military Activity and English Society, 1452–97* (London: RKP, 1981); C. D. Ross, *The Wars of the Roses* (London: Thames and Hudson, 1976), esp. Ch. 4.
5. K. B. McFarlane, 'The Wars of the Roses', in *England in the Fifteenth Century* (London: Hambledon Press, 1981), p. 238.
6. W. Denton, *England in the Fifteenth Century* (London: George Bell, 1888), p. 287.

1 THE WARS IN HISTORY

1. For these views see especially J. R. Lander, 'The Wars of the Roses', in *Crown and Nobility, 1450–1509* (London: Edward Arnold, 1976), pp. 61–3; McFarlane, 'Wars of the Roses', pp. 229, 239; S. B. Chrimes, *Lancastrians, Yorkists and Henry VII* (London: Macmillan, second ed., 1966), p. xii.
2. W. Lamont (ed.), *The Tudors and Stuarts* (London: Sussex Books, 1976), pp. 14–15.
3. M. E. Aston, 'Richard II and the Wars of the Roses', in F. R. H. DuBoulay and C. M. Barron (eds), *The Reign of Richard II: essays in honour of May McKisack* (London: Athlone, 1971), p. 283; Chrimes, *Lancastrians*, p. xii, note 1.

4. A. Raine (ed.), *York Civic Records*, Vol. I (Yorkshire Archaeological Society Record Series, 98, 1939), p. 156.
5. N. Pronay and J. Cox (eds), *The Crowland Chronicle Continuations: 1459–1486* (Richard III and Yorkist History Trust, 1986), pp. 184–185.
6. Aston, loc. cit., pp. 282–4.
7. S. Anglo, *Spectacle, Pageantry and Early Tudor Policy* (Oxford: Clarendon Press, 1969), pp. 18–19.
8. *Rotuli Parliamentorum*, Vol. VI, p. 241.
9. Ibid., Vol. V, p. 464.
10. E. Hall, *The Union of the Two Noble Families of Lancaster and York* (Menston, Scolar Press, 1970), fo. 1.
11. Aston, loc. cit., p. 282–3.
12. Wells, op. cit., pp. 91–115; John Wilders, *The Lost Garden* (London: Macmillan, 1978), pp. 125–51.
13. W. Stubbs, *The Constitutional History of England*, Vol. III, fifth ed. (Oxford: Clarendon Press, 1897), p. 632.
14. Sir George Buck, *The History of King Richard the Third* (1619), A. N. Kincaid (ed.), (Gloucester: Alan Sutton, 1979); H. Walpole, *Historic Doubts on the Life and Reign of Richard III* (London, 1768; reprinted with introduction by P. W. Hammond, Gloucester: Alan Sutton, 1987); C. A. Halsted, *Richard III as Duke of Gloucester and King of England*, 2 vols (London: Longman, 1844).
15. Stubbs, op. cit., Vol. III, p. 632.
16. Sir John Fortescue, *The Governance of England*, Charles Plummer (ed.) (Oxford University Press, 1885), pp. 1–30.
17. Denton, op. cit., pp. 115, 118, 119.
18. Ibid. pp. 260–1.
19. Aston, loc. cit., p. 285.
20. J. R. Green, *A Short History of the English People*, third ed. (London: Macmillan, 1916), pp. 288–90.
21. J. E. T. Rogers, *Six Centuries of Work and Wages* (London: Sonnenschein, 1886), pp. 240–2, 326, 334.
22. C. L. Kingsford, *Prejudice and Promise in Fifteenth Century England* (Oxford University Press, 1925), pp. 48, 63–9.
23. See G. L. Harriss, 'Introduction' in McFarlane, *England in the Fifteenth Century*, esp. p. xix.
24. McFarlane, 'The Wars of the Roses', pp. 231–61.
25. Lander, *Crown and Nobility*, p. 56.
26. Ross, *Wars of the Roses*, p. 176.
27. John Gillingham, *The Wars of the Roses: Peace and Conflict in Fifteenth Century England* (London: Weidenfeld, 1981), pp. 14, 15.

28. R. L. Storey, *The End of the House of Lancaster* (London: Barrie and Rockliff, 1966), pp. 8–28; M. H. Keen, *England in the Late Middle Ages* (London: Methuen, 1973), pp. 449–51.

29. D. M. Loades, *Politics and the Nation, 1450–1660* (Brighton: Harvester, 1974), pp. 11, 100–2.

30. Goodman, *Wars of the Roses*, pp. 3, 218–20.

31. J. C. Wedgwood, *History of Parliament: Biographies of the Members of the Commons House, 1439–1509* (London: HMSO, 1936); J. S. Roskell, *The Commons and Their Speakers in English Parliaments, 1376–1523* (Manchester University Press, 1965). Wedgwood's history is soon to be superceded by a new study of parliament in the fifteenth century edited by J. S. Roskell.

32. Lander, *Crown and Nobility*, p. 94.

33. Goodman, *Wars of the Roses*, pp. 5, 8; McFarlane, 'Wars of the Roses', p. 240; Gillingham, op. cit., p. 254; Ross, *Wars of the Roses*, p. 93.

2   THE COURSE OF THE WARS

1. Unless otherwise noted reference for this narrative should be made to the major political studies of the later-fifteenth century. The reign of Henry VI is comprehensively detailed in R. A. Griffiths, *The Reign of King Henry VI* (London: Ernest Benn, 1981). Part Three, 'The Approach of Civil War 1453–1461', is by far the fullest discussion available of these years. The standard works for Edward IV's reign are C. L. Scofield, *The Life and Reign of Edward IV*, 2 vols (London: Longman, 1923) which provides the greater detail and Charles Ross, *Edward IV* (London: Eyre Methuen, 1974), which offers a corrected and modern interpretation. Charles Ross, *Richard III* (London: Eyre Methuen, 1981), is the fullest and most soundly based of many recent studies. For Henry VII see S. B. Chrimes, *Henry VII* (London: Eyre Methuen, 1972).

2. This point is stressed in A. J. Pollard, 'The Last of the Lancastrians', *Parliamentary History*, 2 (1983), p. 204.

3. I differ from Professor Griffiths (*Henry VI*, pp. 772–808) in dating Queen Margaret's capture of complete control of the Court from November 1458 rather than November 1456.

4. R. A. Griffiths, 'The sense of Dynasty in the Reign of Henry VI', in Charles Ross (ed.), *Patronage, Pedigree and Power in Later Medieval England* (Gloucester: Alan Sutton, 1979), pp. 30–1.

5. J. R. Lander, 'Marriage and Politics in the fifteenth century', in

Crown and Nobility, pp. 94–126 argued that the Woodvilles were not excessively rewarded. M. A. Hicks, 'The Changing Role of the Wydevilles in Yorkist Politics to 1483', in Ross (ed.), *Patronage, Pedigree and Power*, pp. 60–73 concluded that their influence and gains were excessive.

6. A. J. Pollard, 'Lord FitzHugh's Rising in 1470', *Bulletin of the Institute of Historical Research*, 52 (1979), pp. 170–5.
7. R. A. Griffiths and R. S. Thomas, *The Making of the Tudor Dynasty* (Gloucester: Alan Sutton, 1985), p. 85.
8. For a recent suggestion that Somerset's loyalty to Henry VI was the key to his behaviour see M. A. Hicks, 'Edward IV and Lancastrian Loyalism in the North', *Northern History*, 20 (1984), pp. 23–37, esp. p. 29.

3 THE CAUSES OF THE WARS

1. Fortescue, op. cit., pp. 14–15; Denton, op. cit., pp. 273–4.
2. Storey, *House of Lancaster*, pp. 9, 10, 14, 16, 27.
3. M. Prestwich, *The Three Edwards: War and State in England, 1272–1377* (London: Methuen, 1980), pp. 165–244; Keen, *Later Middle Ages*, pp. 143–65.
4. McFarlane, 'Wars of the Roses', p. 238.
5. Ibid., pp. x–xviii.
6. Public Record Office, KB 9/13/23.
7. N. Davis (ed.), *Paston Letters and Papers of the Fifteenth Century*, Part I (Oxford: Clarendon Press, 1971), p. 530; T. Stapleton (ed.), *The Plumpton Correspondence* (London: Camden Society, 1839), pp. 45, 72–3.
8. For recent discussion of arbitration see C. Carpenter, 'Law, Justice and Landowners in Late Medieval England', *Law and History Review*, 1 (1983), pp. 205–37; M. A. Hicks, 'Restraint, mediation and private justice: George, duke of Clarence as "Good Lord"', *Jnl of Legal History*, 4 (1983), pp. 56–71; E. Powell, 'Arbitration and the law in England in the Later Middle Ages', *Trans. Roy. Hist. Soc.*, fifth series, 33 (1983), pp. 49–67; C. Rawcliffe, 'The Great lord as Peacemaker', in J. A. Guy and H. G. Beale (eds), *Law and Social Change in British History* (Royal Historical Society Study in History, 40, 1984); and I. Rowney, 'Arbitration in gentry disputes in the later Middle Ages', *History*, 67 (1982), pp. 367–76.
9. See esp. W. H. Dunham, *Lord Hastings' Indentured Retainers, 1461–*

1483 (Connecticut Academy of Arts and Science, 1955), pp. 7–14.

10. Carpenter, 'Law, Justice and Landowners', pp. 205–37, and 'The Duke of Clarence and the Midlands', *Midland History*, 11 (1986), pp. 23–48; M. Cherry, 'The Courtenay Earls of Devon: the Foundation and Disintegration of a Late-Medieval Aristocratic Affinity', in *Southern History*, 1 (1979), pp. 71–97 and 'The Struggle for Power in Mid-Fifteenth Century Devonshire', in R. A. Griffiths (ed.), *Patronage, the Crown and the Provinces in Later-Medieval England* (Gloucester: Alan Sutton, 1981), pp. 123–44.

11. R. A. Griffiths, 'Local Rivalries and National Politics: the Percies, the Nevilles and the duke of Exeter, 1452–55', *Speculum*, 43, No. 4 (1968), pp. 589–632.

12. McFarlane, 'Wars of the Roses', pp. 250–1, and *Nobility*, pp. 108–109.

13. M. M. Postan, 'The Fifteenth Century', in *Essays in Medieval Agriculture and Economy* (Cambridge University Press, 1973), p. 48; T. B. Pugh and C. D. Ross, 'The English Baronage and the Income Tax of 1436', *Bulletin of the Institute of Historical Research*, 20 (1953), pp. 1–2.

14. McFarlane, *Nobility*, pp. 177–86.

15. T. B. Pugh, *The Marcher Lordships of South Wales, 1415–1536* (Cardiff: University of Wales Press, 1963), pp. 36–43, 143–8; J. T. Rosenthal, 'The Estates and Finances of Richard, duke of York (1411–60)', *Studies in Medieval and Renaissance History*, 2 (1965), pp. 122–46; C. D. Ross, 'The Estates and Finances of Richard, Duke of York', *Welsh History Review*, III (1966–67), pp. 299–302.

16. McFarlane, *Nobility*, pp. 186, 213–27.

17. See my forthcoming work on north-eastern England in the fifteenth century to be published by Oxford University Press.

18. Griffiths, *Henry VI*, pp. 582–3.

19. B. P. Wolffe, *The Royal Demesne in English History* (London: George Allen, 1971), pp. 76–123; Griffiths, *Henry VI*, pp. 376–401, 785–9.

20. McFarlane, 'Wars of the Roses', pp. 239–40; Keen, *Later Middle Ages*, pp. 456, 513.

21. C. F. Richmond, '1485 and All That', in P. W. Hammond (ed.), *Richard III: Lordship, Loyalty and Law* (Gloucester: Alan Sutton, 1986), pp. 186–8.

22. M. H. Keen, *Chivalry* (Newhaven: Yale University Press, 1984), esp. pp. 143–78, 238–53.

23. A. B. Ferguson, *The Indian Summer of English Chivalry* (Durham N.C.: Duke University Press, 1960), pp. 144–53.

24. J. R. Lander, *Government and Community: England, 1450–1509*

(London: Edward Arnold, 1950), p. 160; A. Goodman, 'Responses to requests in Yorkshire for military service under Henry V', *Northern History*, 17 (1981), pp. 240–52; D. A. L. Morgan, 'The Individual Style of the English Gentleman', in Michael Jones (ed.), *Gentry and Lesser Nobility in Later Medieval Europe* (Gloucester: Alan Sutton, 1986), pp. 15–35.

25. A. R. Myers, *England in the Later Middle Ages* (London: Penguin, 1952), p. 140.

26. McFarlane, 'Wars of the Roses', p. 240; B. P. Wolffe, *Henry VI* (London: Eyre Methuen, 1981), pp. 211–12.

27. K. B. McFarlane, 'The War, the Economy and Social Change' and 'The Investment of Sir John Fastolf's Profits of War', in *England in the Fifteenth Century*, pp. 139–50, 175–98; *Nobility*, pp. 19–40.

28. C. T. Allmand and C. A. J. Armstrong (eds), *English Suits before the Parlement of Paris, 1420–36*, (Camden: fourth series, 26, 1982), pp. 291–2, *CPR, 1446–52*, p. 470; A. J. Pollard, *John Talbot and the War in France, 1427–1453* (Royal Historical Society Study in History, 35, 1983), p. 120.

29. Ibid., pp. 109–11; Griffiths, *Henry VI*, pp. 404–6.

30. Storey, *House of Lancaster*, p. 73. I owe some of these ideas on York to Dr Michael Jones.

31. Griffiths, *Henry VI*, pp. 669–74.

32. Keen, *Later Middle Ages*, pp. 456, 513.

33. Griffiths, 'The Sense of Dynasty', pp. 23–5.

34. T. B. Pugh, 'The Southampton Plot of 1415', in R. A. Griffiths and J. W. Sherborne (eds), *Kings and Nobles in the Later Middle Ages* (Gloucester: Alan Sutton, 1986), pp. 69–76.

35. For the following paragraphs see Griffiths, *Henry VI*, esp. pp. 240–253; Wolffe, *Henry VI*; and Roger Lovatt, 'A Collector of Apocryphal Anecdotes: John Blacman Revisited', in A. J. Pollard (ed.), *Property and Politics: Essays in Later Medieval English History* (Gloucester: Alan Sutton, 1984), pp. 172–97.

36. Wolffe, *Henry VI*, pp. 125–32.

37. Lovatt, loc. cit., pp. 172–97 passim.

38. Griffiths, *Henry VI*, pp. 776–7; Wolffe, *Henry VI*, pp. 182–3, 303.

39. McFarlane, 'Wars of the Roses', p. 239.

40. Ross, *Edward IV*, pp. 134, 406–7.

41. D. A. L. Morgan, 'The King's Affinity in the Polity of Yorkist England', *Trans. Roy. Hist. Soc.*, fifth series, 23 (1973), pp. 1–25.

42. Ross, *Richard III*, pp. 44–62; Rosemary Horrox (ed.), *Richard III and the North* (University of Hull, Studies in Regional and Local History, 6, 1986), passim.

43. C. Rawcliffe, *The Staffords, Earls of Stafford and Dukes of Buckingham, 1394–1521* (Cambridge University Press, 1978), pp. 28–9.
44. D. E. Lowe, 'Patronage and Politics: Edward IV, the Wydevilles and the Council of the Prince of Wales', *Bulletin of the Board of Celtic Studies*, 29 (1981), pp. 270–3.
45. Richmond, '1485 and All That', pp. 186–91.
46. R. H. Helmholtz, 'The Sons of Edward IV: A Canonical Assessment of the Claim that they were Illegitimate', in Hammond (ed.) *Richard III: Lordship, Loyalty and Law*, p. 92.
47. This is the theme of Dominic Mancini's, *Occupatione*, written before the end of 1483. See C. A. J. Armstrong (ed.), *The Usurpation of Richard III* (Oxford: Clarendon Press, second ed., 1969).
48. M. A. Hicks, *Richard III as duke of Gloucester: a study in Character* (York: Borthwick Paper, No. 70, 1986).
49. Charles T. Wood, 'Richard III, William, Lord Hastings and Friday the Thirteenth', in Griffiths and Sherborne (eds), *Kings and Nobles*, pp. 155–68.
50. Lorraine C. Attreed, 'From *Pearl* Maiden to Tower princes', *Journal of Medieval History*, 9 (1983), pp. 52–5.
51. Anne F. Sutton, 'A Curious searcher for our Weal Public', in Hammond (ed.), *Richard III: Lordship, Loyalty and Law*, pp. 58–90.
52. A. H. Thomas and I. D. Thornley (eds), *The Great Chronicle of London* (London, 1938), p. 238.

4 THE SCALE OF THE WARS

1. Lander, *Crown and Nobility*, p. 62; Dunham, op. cit., pp. 24–5.
2. Goodman, *Wars of the Roses*, pp. 227–8.
3. Ross, *Wars of the Roses*, pp. 135–6.
4. Ibid., pp. 138–40.
5. McFarlane, 'Wars of the Roses', p. 244; T. B. Pugh, 'The Magnates, Knights and the Gentry', in S. B. Chrimes et al. (eds), *Fifteenth-Century England* (Manchester University Press, 1972), p. 110; Lander, *Crown and Nobility*, p. 24; and *Government and Community*, pp. 278, 326.
6. Ross, *Wars of the Roses*, p. 144; *Richard III*, pp. 157–69.
7. Ross, *Edward IV*, p. 157.
8. Pugh, 'The Magnates', p. 114; Lander, *Crown and Nobility*, p. 25; C. F. Richmond, '1485 and All That', p. 173; Ross, *Richard III*, pp. 158–62, 235–7.

9. Ross, *Richard III*, pp. 212–26, Richmond, '1485 and All That', p. 174.
10. McFarlane, 'Wars of the Roses', pp. 248–54.
11. Ibid., p. 254; M. A. Hicks, *False, Fleeting Perjur'd Clarence: George Duke of Clarence, 1449–78* (Gloucester: Alan Sutton, 1980), pp. 183–4, 243. Hicks states that Vernon did not turn out.
12. Ross, *Edward IV*, pp. 318–22; *Richard III*, p. 133.
13. R. L. Storey, 'The north of England', in Chrimes et al. (eds), *Fifteenth-century England* pp. 138–42; A. J. Pollard, 'St Cuthbert and the Hog: Richard III and the County Palatine of Durham, 1471–85', in Griffiths and Sherborne (eds), *Kings and Nobles*, pp. 114–23.
14. C. S. L. Davies, 'Bishop Morton, the Holy See, and the Accession of Henry VII', *English Historical Review*, 102, 1 (1987), pp. 24–5.
15. Above p. 24–5; Ross, *Edward IV*, pp. 145–6, 173–4; N. Pronay and J. Cox (eds), op. cit., p. 155.
16. Thomas More, *Utopia* (Complete Works, Vol. 4, Yale University Press, 1965) p. 63; Stubbs, op. cit., Vol. III, p. 559; Green, *Short History*, p. 302; Storey, *House of Lancaster*, p. 9.
17. A. R. Myers (ed.), *The Household of Edward IV* (Manchester University Press, 1959), p. 90ff.
18. Hicks, *Clarence*, p. 185; Rawcliffe, *Staffords*, pp. 68–9; T. Percy, *The Northumberland Household Book* (London: privately published, 1777), pp. 45, 157.
19. J. P. Collier (ed.), *Household Books of John Duke of Norfolk* (London: Roxburghe Club, 1844), pp. 445–53.
20. Myers, *Household*, p. 116; Collier, op. cit., pp. 453–5.
21. Dunham, op. cit., pp. 27–9.
22. Rawcliffe, *Staffords*, pp. 73–4; A. Compton Reeves, 'Some of Humphrey Stafford's Military Indentures', *Nottingham Medieval Studies*, 16 (1972), pp. 80–7.
23. Davis (ed.), op. cit. Part II, p. 532.
24. J. Gairdner (ed.), *The Historical Collections of a Citizen of London* (Camden Society, 1876), p. 204.
25. Ibid., pp. 209–10.
26. Hicks, *Clarence*, p. 183; Shropshire Record Office, Bridgwater Papers, 87, Receiver's Account for 1470–1.
27. Collier, op. cit., pp. 480–93.
28. Gairdner, *Historical Collections*, p. 212.
29. Ross, *Edward IV*, pp. 23–4; 124–5.
30. McFarlane, 'Wars of the Roses', p. 254; Ross, *Edward IV*, p. 132.

31. C. F. Richmond, 'Fauconberg's Kentish Rising of May 1471', *English Historical Review*, 85 (1970), pp. 673–92.

32. A. J. Pollard, 'The Richmondshire Community of Gentry during the Wars of the Roses', in Ross (ed.), *Patronage, Pedigree and Power*, pp. 37–42.

33. J. Nicolson and R. Burn, *History of Westmorland and Cumberland* (London: Strachan and Cadell, 1777), pp. 96–7; Durham Record Office, D/St 34/ 27–28 Henry VI.

34. Public Record Office, E 28/79/65, 159/238; *York City Records*, Vol. I, pp. 34–6, 39–42, 54, 57–64; Durham, Dean and Chapter, Bursar's Accounts, 1480–1, 1482–3; Historical Manuscripts Commission, *Report on the MSS of Beverley* (HMSO, 1901), pp. 107–8, 116–17, 133–4; J. Raine (ed.), *The Priory of Hexham*, Vol. I (Surtees Society, 44, 1864), pp. cvii–viii.

35. Public Record Office, Durh 3/55/8.

36. J. Gairdner (ed.), *Paston Letters 1422–1509*, Vol. III (London: Chatto and Windus, 1904), p. 30.

37. See above, pp. 26–7, 30–1, 38.

38. Scofield, op. cit., Vol. I, pp. 135–6.

39. A. J. Pollard, 'North, South and Richard III', *The Ricardian*, 5, 74 (1981), pp. 384–9; R. Steele, *Tudor and Stuart Proclamations*, Vol. I (Oxford University Press, 1910), No. 19.

40. McFarlane, 'Wars of the Roses', p. 241.

41. A. J. Pollard, 'The tyranny of Richard III', *Journal of Medieval History*, 3 (1971), pp. 158–63.

42. Pronay and Cox, op. cit., p. 191; D. Hay (ed.), *The 'Anglica Historia' of Polydore Vergil* (Camden Series, 1950), p. 11.

43. Philippe de Commynes, *Memoirs: the reign of Louis XI, 1461–83*, transl. Michael Jones (London: Penguin, 1972), p. 345.

44. McFarlane, 'Wars of the Roses', p. 242.

45. Lander, *Crown and Nobility*, pp. 62–4.

46. Goodman, *Wars of the Roses*, pp. 218–20; Durham, Church Commission, 189875, 189817.

47. Griffiths, *Henry VI*, pp. 811–14; Ross, *Edward IV*, pp. 45–6, 49–50, 53–7.

48. Griffiths, *Henry VI*, pp. 886–90; Ross, *Edward IV*, pp. 104–114.

49. Griffiths, *Henry VI*, pp. 890–1; Ross, *Edward IV*, pp. 146–7, 158–60; J. R. Lander, 'The Hundred Years' War and Edward IV's 1475 campaign in France', in *Crown and Nobility*, pp. 227–8.

50. Ross, *Edward IV*, pp. 288–90.

51. A. V. Antonovics, 'Henry VII, King of England, By the Grace of

Charles VIII of France', in Griffiths and Sherborne (eds), *Kings and Nobles*, pp. 169–84.

5 AFTERMATH AND THE WIDER CONTEXT OF THE WARS

1. Green, op. cit., pp. 289–92; A. F. Pollard, *Factors in Modern History*, third ed. (London: Constable, 1932), pp. 32–51.
2. Aston, loc. cit., pp. 290–1.
3. McFarlane, *Nobility*, pp. 142–67, 172–6.
4. M. A. Hicks, 'Counting the Cost of War: the Moleyns Ransom and the Hungerford Land Sales, 1453–87', *Southern History*, 8 (1986), p. 28.
5. J. R. Lander, 'Attainder and Forfeiture, 1453–1509', in *Crown and Nobility*, pp. 127–58; M. A. Hicks, 'Attainder, Resumption and Coercion, 1461–1529', *Parliamentary History*, 3 (1984), pp. 15–31.
6. McFarlane, 'Wars of the Roses', pp. 260–1.
7. Wolffe, *Royal Demesne*, pp. 158–79; Ross, *Edward IV*, pp. 371–87; Chrimes, *Henry VII*, Part II passim and pp. 194–218; B. P. Wolffe, *Yorkist and Early Tudor Government, 1461–1509*, (Historical Association, 1966).
8. Wolffe, *Royal Demesne*, pp. 143–225; Alexander Grant, *Henry VII: the importance of his reign in English history* (London: Methuen, 1985), pp. 42–5.
9. J. S. Roskell, *The Impeachment of Michael de La Pole, Earl of Suffolk in 1386* (Manchester University Press, 1984), pp. 30–5.
10. Griffiths, *Henry VI*, pp. 825–6.
11. For these points see G. L. Harriss, 'Medieval Government and Statecraft', *Past and Present*, 25 (1963), pp. 8–38, and D. Starkey, 'The Age of the Household: politics, society and the arts, c.1350–1550', in S. Medcalf (ed.), *The Later Middle Ages: the context of English Literature* (London: Methuen, 1981), pp. 227–89.
12. Morgan, loc. cit., pp. 1–25; Ross, *Edward IV* pp. 388–413.
    England', *Trans. Roy. Hist. Soc.* fifth series, 23 (1973), pp. 1–25;
13. Grant, *Henry VII*, p. 19.
14. Ibid., pp. 12, 23.
15. Chrimes, *Henry VII*, pp. 208–12; Rawcliffe, *Staffords*, p. 36; M. E. Condon, 'Ruling Elites in the Reign of Henry VII', in Charles Ross (ed.), *Patronage, Pedigree and Power*, p. 119.
16. Grant, *Henry VII*, pp. 28–31.

17. Condon, loc. cit., pp. 116–19.

18. This topic will be discussed further in my forthcoming study of north-eastern England in the later fifteenth century.

19. J. Gairdner (ed.), *Letters and Papers Illustrative of the reigns of Richard III and Henry VII*, Vol. II (HMSO, Rolls series, 1863), p. 84.

20. Condon, loc. cit., pp. 121, 129.

21. C. S. L. Davies, *Peace, Print and Protestantism, 1450–1558* (London: Hart Davis, 1976), p. 104.

22. Grant, *Henry VII*, pp. 46–50.

23. For Scotland see, J. Brown (ed.), *Scottish Society in the Fifteenth Century* (London: Edward Arnold, 1977); Grant, *Independence and Nationhood: Scotland 1306–1469* (London: Edward Arnold, 1984); N. McDougall, *James III* (Edinburgh: John Donald, 1982); R. Nicholson, *Scotland: the Later Middle Ages* (Edinburgh:Oliver and Boyd, 1974); and J. Wormald, *Court, Kirk and Community: Scotland, 1470–1625* (London: Edward Arnold, 1974).

24. N. McDougall, 'Richard III and James III: Contemporary Monarchs and Contemporary Mythologies', in Hammond (ed.), *Richard III, Lordship, Loyalty and Law*, pp. 148–71.

25. Grant, *Independence and Nationhood*, p. 199.

26. The standard introduction in English to late-medieval French Society is P. S. Lewis, *Later Medieval France: The Polity*, (London: Macmillan, 1968).

27. Until the publication of M. G. A. Vale's forthcoming volume on later-medieval France there is no up-to-date account of the whole of its early-fifteenth century history. Recent detailed studies in English to which reference should be made include R. Vaughan, *John the Fearless: the Growth of Burgundian Power* (London: Longman, 1966) and *Philip the Good: the Apogee of Burgundy* (London: Longman, 1970); M. G. A. Vale, *Charles VII* (London: Eyre Methuen, 1974), and C. T. Allmand, *Lancastrian Normandy, 1415–50* (Oxford: Clarendon Press, 1983).

28. See P. M. Kendall, *Louis XI* (London: Allen Unwin, 1971); Vaughan, *Philip the Good; Charles the Bold* (London: Longman, 1973); and *Valois Burgundy* (London: Alan Lane, 1975).

29. Until the publication of A. V. Antonovics' *Charles VIII*, the best available account is J. C. Bridge, *A History of France from the death of Louis XI*, Vol. 1, *Reign of Charles VIII, Regency of Anne of Beaujeu, 1483–1493*, (Oxford: Clarendon Press, 1921). For the Netherlands see C. A. J. Armstrong, 'The Burgundian Netherlands 1477–1521', *New Cambridge Modern History*, Vol. 1 (1967), pp. 224–42.

30. This paragraph is based on J. N. Hilgarth, *The Spanish Kingdoms*,

1250–1576, Vol. II, *1410–1516*, (Oxford University Press, 1978), pp. 271–97; 317–41; 351–63.

31. Ibid., pp. 318–22, 342–7.
32. Commynes, *Memoirs*, p. 90.

SELECT BIBLIOGRAPHY

This bibliography is designed to provide an introductory guide to secondary works relevant to the Wars of the Roses, especially those that are historiographically significant and illustrate recent trends in scholarship. For works on Scotland, France and Spain the reader should see the references to Chapter 5, notes 23 and 26–30 inclusive. Fuller bibliographies are to be found in Griffiths, *Henry VI* and Ross, *Edward IV* and *Richard III* (see below). De Lloyd J. Guth, *England 1377–1485* (Cambridge University Press, 1976) is an excellent bibliography of works up to that date. For comprehensive listing of more recent works the reader should consult The Royal Historical Society's annual *Bibliography of British and Irish History*.

C. A. J. Armstrong, 'Politics and the battle of St Albans, 1455', *Bulletin of the Institute of Historical Research*, 33 (1960), pp. 1–72 – the battle dissected.

M. E. Aston, 'Richard II and the Wars of the Roses', in C. M. Barron and F. R. H. Du Boulay (eds), *The Reign of Richard II* (London: Athlone Press, 1971), pp. 280–317 – contains the best discussion of the elaboration of the idea of the Wars of the Roses in the sixteenth century.

A. Cameron, 'The giving of livery and retaining in Henry VII's reign', *Renaissance and Modern Studies*, 18 (1974), pp. 17–35 – a perceptive reconsideration of Henry VII's policy towards bastard feudalism.

C. Carpenter, 'Law, Justice and Landowners in Late Medieval England', *Law and History Review*, 1 (1983), pp. 205–37.

——, 'The Duke of Clarence and the Midlands: a study in the interplay of local and national politics', *Midland History*, 11 (1986), pp. 23–48.

——, two articles, drawing on the author's doctoral thesis on Warwickshire in the fifteenth century, which illuminate local rivalries in the midlands.

M. Cherry, 'The Struggle for Power in Mid-Fifteenth Century Devonshire', in R. A. Griffiths (ed.), *Patronage, the Crown and Provinces in Later Medieval England* (Gloucester: Alan Sutton, 1981), pp. 123–44 – the most recent consideration of the Bonville–Courtenay feud in the west country.

S. B. Chrimes, *Henry VII* (London: Eyre Methuen, 1972) – the standard modern study, strong on government.

——, *Lancastrians, Yorkists and Henry VII* (London: Macmillan, second ed. 1966) – one of the first surveys to dispense with the idea of the Wars of the Roses.

M. E. Condon, 'Ruling Elites in the Reign of Henry VII', in Charles Ross (ed.), *Patronage, Pedigree and Power* (Gloucester: Alan Sutton, 1979), pp. 109–42 – an excellent analysis of Henry VII's regime.

W. Denton, *England in the Fifteenth Century* (London: George Bell, 1888) – the most extreme expression of the nineteenth-century gloss to traditional views.

W. H. Dunham, *Lord Hastings Indentured Retainers, 1461–83* (Connecticut Academy of Arts and Science, 39, 1955) – a pioneering study of a bastard feudal retinue, many conclusions of which have since been modified.

J. Gillingham, *The Wars of the Roses: Peace and Conflict in Fifteenth-Century England* (London: Weidenfeld and Nicolson, 1981) – a full narrative account, a particular feature being its emphasis on the peaceful nature of fifteenth-century England – the opposite pole to Denton.

A. Goodman, *The Wars of the Roses: Military Activity and English Society, 1452–97* (London: RKP, 1981) – a companion to Gillingham which concentrates on military aspects and views the wars as being more disruptive.

A. Grant, *Henry VII: the importance of his reign in English history* (London: Methuen, 1985) – the most recent and best available introduction to the subject.

J. R. Green, *A Short History of the English People* (London: Macmillan, third ed., 1918) – the inventor of New Monarchy.

R. A. Griffiths, *The Reign of King Henry VI* (London: Ernest Benn, 1981) – supercedes all else on the political history of the 1450s, especially the years 1455–61.

——, 'Local Rivalries and National Politics: the Percies, Nevilles and the Duke of Exeter, 1452–1455', *Speculum*, 43 (1968), pp. 589–632 – a comprehensive account of the private war in Yorkshire.

R. A. Griffiths and R. S. Thomas, *The Making of the Tudor Dynasty*

(Gloucester: Alan Sutton, 1985) – indispensable for Henry VII before he became king.

M. A. Hicks, 'Dynastic Change and Northern Society: the career of the Fourth Earl of Northumberland, 1470–89', *Northern History*, 14 (1978) – the standard account of the man accused of betraying Richard III at Bosworth.

——, 'The Changing Role of the Wydevilles in Yorkist Politics to 1483', in Ross (ed.) *Patronage, Pedigree and Power* – the malignity of the Woodvilles restated.

——, *False, Fleeting, Perjur'd Clarence: George, duke of Clarence 1449–1478* (Gloucester: Alan Sutton, 1980) – Clarence's career sensitively considered.

——, *Richard III as Duke of Gloucester: a Study in Character* (Borthwick Papers 70, University of York, 1986) – a controversial assessment of the character, but new light on the political circumstances in 1483.

R. E. Horrox (ed.), *Richard III and the North* (Hull: Studies in Regional and Local History 6, 1986) – a useful collection of essays exploring the northern dimension to Richard III.

Michael Jones, 'Richard III and the Stanleys', in Horrox (ed.) *Richard III and the North* – the best of a clutch of recent assessments of the most successful political family of the Wars of the Roses.

M. H. Keen, *England in the Later Middle Ages* (London: Methuen, 1977) – the best available textbook.

C. L. Kingsford, 'Social Life and the Wars of the Roses', in *Prejudice and Promise in Fifteenth-century England* (Oxford, 1925), pp. 48–77 – the seminal launch of revisionism.

W. Lamont (ed.), *The Tudors and Stuarts* (London: Sussex Books, 1976) – contains the ultimate word on abolishing the Wars of the Roses.

J. R. Lander, *Crown and Nobility, 1450–1509* (London: Edward Arnold, 1976) – a collection of the essays of one of the most influential of modern writers. See especially 'The Wars of the Roses', 'Marriage and Politics', 'Attainder and Forfeiture' and 'Bonds, Coercion and Fear'.

——, *Government and Community: England 1450–1509* (London: Edward Arnold, 1980) – a summation of a life's work, which tends to overrate Edward IV.

R. Lovatt, 'A collector of Apocryphal Anecdotes: John Blacman Revisited', in A. J. Pollard (ed.), *Property and Politics: Essays in Later Medieval History* (Gloucester: Alan Sutton, 1984), pp. 172–97 – a convincing justification of Blacman's portrait of Henry VI.

K. B. McFarlane, *The Nobility of Later Medieval England* (Oxford University Press, 1973) – the authoritative account of the subject, and essential for any consideration of the political élite.

K. B. McFarlane, *England in the Fifteenth Century*, G. L. Harriss (ed.) (London: Hambledon Press, 1981) – a collection of essays including 'Bastard Feudalism' and 'The Wars of the Roses' which are essential starting points; and an introduction which not only charts McFarlane's intellectual pilgrimage but also offers a perceptive analysis of the state of the art.

D. A. L. Morgan, 'The King's Affinity in the Policy of Yorkist England', *Transactions of the Royal Historical Society*, fifth series, 23 (1973), pp. 1–25 – an influential analysis of the Yorkist regime, which underlies most subsequent contrasts with Henry VII.

A. J. Pollard, 'The Tyranny of Richard III', *Journal of Medieval History*, 3 (1977), pp. 147–66 – emphasises the regional character of Richard III's reign.

——, 'The Richmondshire Community of Gentry during the Wars of the Roses', in Ross (ed.), *Patronage, Pedigree and Power*, pp. 37–59.

——, 'St Cuthbert and the Hog: Richard III and the County Palatine of Durham', in R. A. Griffiths and J. W. Sherborne (eds), *Kings and Nobles in Later Medieval England* (Gloucester: Alan Sutton, 1986), pp. 109–29 – two more local studies.

T. B. Pugh, 'The Magnates, Knights and Gentry', in S. B. Chrimes et al. (eds), *Fifteenth-Century England, 1399–1509: studies in Politics and Society* (Manchester University Press, 1972) pp. 86–128 – a valuable analysis of the social structure of the political nation.

C. Rawcliffe, *The Staffords, Earls of Stafford and Dukes of Buckingham, 1394–1521* (Cambridge University Press, 1978) – an excellent baronial case study.

C. F. Richmond, 'The Nobility and the Wars of the Roses, 1459–61', *Nottingham Medieval Studies*, 21 (1977) – a detailed analysis of noble participation in the first stage of the wars.

——, *John Hopton* (Cambridge University Press, 1981) – a fascinating study of one man whom the wars passed by, made all the more intriguing by the recent discovery that he became blind.

——, '1485 and all that, or what was going on at the battle of Bosworth', in P. W. Hammond (ed.), *Richard III: Loyalty, Lordship and Law* (Richard III and Yorkist History Trust, 1986), pp. 172–202 – provocative discussion of Bosworth and more.

C. D. Ross, *Edward IV* (London: Eyre Methuen, 1974) – the standard modern study of the reign.

——, *The Wars of the Roses: a concise history* (London: Thames and Hudson, 1976) – an excellent short introduction, splendidly illustrated.

——, *Richard III* (London: Eyre Methuen, 1981) – the best of several recent studies, skilfully summing up the product of modern scholarship.

I. Rowney, 'Government and Patronage in the Fifteenth Century: Staffordshire, 1439–59', *Midland History*, 8 (1983), pp. 49–69.

——, 'The Hastings Affinity in Staffordshire and the Honour of Tutbury', *Bulletin of the Institute of Historical Research*, 57 (1984). – Two further examples of recent local studies.

A. L. Rowse, *Bosworth Field and the Wars of the Roses* (London: Macmillan, 1966) – the last flowering of the Tudor version of fifteenth-century history.

C. L. Scofield, *The Life and Reign of Edward IV*, 2 vols (London, 1923) – still the most detailed narrative available.

R. L. Storey, *The End of the House of Lancaster* (London: Barrie and Rockliff, 1966) – despite its title, mainly a detailed account of politics 1450–56 and important for its controversial explanation of the wars.

——, 'Lincolnshire and the Wars of the Roses', *Nottingham Medieval Studies*, 14 (1970), pp. 64–82 – more local feuding.

W. Stubbs, *The Constitutional History of England*, Vol. III, fifth ed. (Oxford: Clarendon Press, 1897) – the standard Victorian interpretation of the fifteenth century.

B. P. Wolffe, *Yorkist and Early Tudor Government, 1461–1509* (Historical Association, 1966) – a clear, brief introduction to the subject.

——, *The Royal Demesne in English History* (London: George Allen, 1971) – contains the definitive study of chamber finance.

——, *Henry VI* (London: Eyre Methuen, 1981) – a lively if controversial view of Henry VI's personality.

C. T. Wood, 'Richard III, William Lord Hastings and Friday the Thirteenth', in Griffiths and Sherborne (eds), *Kings and Nobles*, pp. 155–68 – the 'cock-up theory' of history applied to Richard III.

S. M. Wright, *The Derbyshire Gentry in the Fifteenth Century* (Derbyshire Record Society, 8, 1983) – a county study representative of recent research.

GLOSSARY

Affinity   the following of a lord

Annuity   a grant of an annual payment for life or a number of years made by a lord to a *Retainer*

Appanage   the landed estate of a royal prince, often accompanied by extensive legal privileges

Attainder   the parliamentary act of attainting (corrupting the blood) whereby a person guilty of treason loses all civil rights including the right to inherit or hold property

Banneret   a knight entitled to bear a banner; of higher status than a bachelor, a young or junior knight

Bond   a binding agreement; see *Recognisance*

Chamber   the financial office of the royal household; thus chamber finance, the system of managing royal finances from the chamber rather than the *Exchequer*

Chancery   the chief executive and secretarial office of the Crown, housed at Westminster

Demesne   the estate and lands held by the owner himself; hence Royal Demesne, the Crown lands

Enfeoffment to use   a kind of trust in which land is held by trustees on behalf of its owner, often to escape the effect of *Wardship*

Exchequer   the chief financial office of state, housed at Westminster

Felony   a serious crime

131

Heir apparent   the declared heir to the throne, normally the king's eldest son

Heir presumptive   the presumed heir in the event of the king dying without an *Heir apparent*

Indenture   a form of contract between two parties in which each kept a half cut along an indented line; hence Indentured *Retainer*, one who is retained in service by means of such a contract

Livery   the distinctive clothing (a uniform) bestowed by a lord on his *Retainer*

March, marches   border, borders; hence marcher lordships (in Wales) in which lords enjoyed royal privileges and had exclusive jurisdiction

Palatinate   territory under the rule of a count palatine who enjoyed royal privileges and exclusive jurisdiction in it

Readeption   literally the reattainment (of the throne by Henry VI in 1470)

Recognisance   a sum of money pledged as surety by a *Bond* for the future performance of an act or the avoidance of an offence, which is forfeited if the act is not performed or the offence is committed

Retainer   one who is attached in the service of a lord by *Annuity* or *Indenture*

Tenant-in-chief   one who holds land directly from the king as distinct from a lesser lord

Vassal   one who holds land from a lord on condition of allegiance

Wardship   control and use of the lands of a tenant who is a minor and guardianship of the infant heir (including the right to arrange marriage) until that heir has attained his or her majority

INDEX

Index

Losecoat Field, battle of (1470) viii, 30

Louis XI of France 34, 91–3, 107–8

Louis of Orleans 108

Lovell, Viscount 78

Ludford, battle of (1459) viii, 86

Lumley, Lord 77–8, 79

McFarlane, K. B. 2, 14, 15, 18, 49, 51, 52, 54, 56, 58, 59, 64, 76, 77, 80, 88, 89, 96

Magdalen College School, Oxford 3

Maine 63

March, Earl of (*afterwards* Duke of York *and* Edward IV *q.v.*) 6, 25, 26–7, 61

Margaret of Anjou, Queen
domestic affairs 21, 99;
part in wars 21–7 *passim*, 31, 32, 33, 41, 62, 64, 85, 87, 88, 91–2

Margaret of York (Burgundy) 39, 92, 93

Mary of Guelders 88, 91

Masham, Lord 78

Maximilian of Austria 107–8

Moleyn family 42

Montagu, John, Lord *see under* Northumberland, Earls of

Monthéry, battle of viii, 107

More, Sir Thomas and *UTOPIA: History of King Richard III* 11, 82, 95

Morgan, Dr 67

Mortimer, Edmund *see* March, Earl of; Edward IV

Mortimer's Cross, battle of (1461) viii, 26

Morton, John, Bishop of Ely 34, 36, 80

Mulso, Sir Edmund 60

Netherlands 29

Neville family x, 22, 23, 24, 80, 86–7, 96, 102
feuds 42, 43–4, 67

Neville, Anne 31, 35

Neville, George, Bishop of Exeter and Archbishop of York 80

Neville, George, Duke of Bedford 71

Neville, Sir Humphrey 30, 44

Neville, Sir John 44, 85

Neville, Ralph *see under* Westmorland, Earls of

Neville, Richard *see under* Salisbury, Earl of; Warwick, Earls of

Neville, Richard, Lord Latimer 96

Neville, Robert, Bishop of Durham 81

Neville, Sir Thomas 85

New Yorkists 28

Nibley Green, battle of (1470) viii, 65

Nicolas, Sir Harry: *Proceedings of the Privy Council* (1836) 12

Norfolk, John, Lord Howard, Duke of 36, 52, 65, 83–4, 85

Norham, siege of (1463) viii, 91

Normandy 21, 56, 58, 59, 60, 61, 107

Northampton, battle of (1460) viii, 25

Northumberland, Earls of 83
2nd Earl (d. 1455) 22, 23, 59
3rd Earl (d. 1461) 43–4
John, Lord Montagu, 4th Earl (d. 1471) 27, 31, 32, 44, 52, 87
Henry Percy, 5th Earl (d. 1489)
in wars 23, 26, 32, 36, 38, 78;
personal and domestic affairs 39, 54, 55, 101, 102

Oglander, Sir John 6

Oldhall, Sir William 57, 60

Orleans, Dukes of 106, 107, 108

Oxford, Earl of 33, 79, 100, 101

Parliament of Devils 25

Paston family 42, 52, 80
the Paston Letters 11–12

Paston, Sir John 52, 65

Pembroke, Earls of
Lord Herbert 1st Earl (d. 1469) 26, 28, 30
Jasper Tudor 33, 79, 92, 100
William, 2nd Earl (d. 1491) 78

Percy family *see also*
Northumberland, Earls of 42, 43–4, 67, 80, 86–7, 96

Percy, Henry *see under* Northumberland, Earls of

Philip The Good of Burgundy 91

Plummer, Charles 12, 14, 46, 50

Plumpton family 52, 80

136